KNOWLEDGE MEANS EMPOWERMENT.
TEST YOURSELF.

1. Lack of sexual desire in women usually indicates a hormone imbalance. True or false?

2. As many as 20% of women have never had an orgasm with sexual activity. True or false?

3. What is the biggest sexual problem of post-menopausal women? Is it easy to treat?

4. What sexually transmitted diseases often have NO symptoms?

5. Is there a link between genital warts and cancer?

6. Currently, who is at greater risk of contracting HIV, heterosexuals or homosexuals?

ISN'T IT IMPORTANT THAT YOU HAVE THE FACTS? YOUR LIFE AND YOUR HEALTH MAY DEPEND ON THEM.

Answers:

1. *False. It is most often caused by a problem in the relationship.*
2. *True. But virtually all can if they get proper treatment.*
3. *Vaginal dryness. It is very easy to treat.*
4. *Chlamydia, gonorrhea, and CMV.*
5. *Yes.*
6. *Heterosexuals.*

Other books by the American Medical Women's Association

THE WOMEN'S COMPLETE HEALTHBOOK
THE AMWA GUIDE TO NUTRITION AND
WELLNESS
THE AMWA GUIDE TO PREGNANCY AND
CHILDBIRTH
THE AMWA GUIDE TO FERTILITY AND
REPRODUCTIVE HEALTH
THE AMWA GUIDE TO EMOTIONAL HEALTH

The American Medical Women's Association

Guide to
Sexuality

Medical Co-editors
**Roselyn Payne Epps, M.D., M.P.H.,
M.A., F.A.A.P.
Susan Cobb Stewart, M.D., F.A.C.P.**

A Dell Book

Published by
Dell Publishing
a division of
Bantam Doubleday Dell Publishing Group, Inc.
1540 Broadway
New York, New York 10036

This material was originally published along with other material
in THE WOMEN'S COMPLETE HEALTHBOOK published by
Delacorte Press.

Illustrations by Wendy Frost

ISBN: 0-440-22249-4

Reprinted by arrangement with Delacorte Press

Printed in the United States of America

Published simultaneously in Canada

October 1996

10 9 8 7 6 5 4 3 2 1

OPM

The AMWA Guide to Sexuality

Roselyn Payne Epps, M.D., M.P.H., M.A.,
and Susan Cobb Stewart, M.D.

Sexuality is not only a requirement for the perpetuation of life, but it is also a major element of emotional fulfillment, physical enjoyment, and intimacy between lovers. A woman's sexual well-being depends on both emotional and physical health—from puberty to menopause and beyond. The sexual revolution that began in the 1960s has enabled women to be open and free with their sexual desires. In the 1990s, women must understand that with freedom comes responsibility: to avoid unwanted pregnancy and to avoid the spread of sexually transmitted diseases. *The AMWA Guide to Sexuality* presents essential information developed by the American Medical Women's Association (AMWA), the most historic and prestigious association of women physicians in the world. The authors are all women physicians with an in-depth understanding of female sexuality.

AMWA believes that women must avoid a disease-oriented approach to women's health and focus on maintaining optimal health on a daily and long-term basis. The more a woman knows about her body and its functions, the better equipped she will be to safeguard good health through preventive strategies such as using contraceptives and knowing the signs of sexually transmitted diseases.

The content of *The AMWA Guide to Sexuality* is divided into four major sections: Part I, Sexuality, describes healthy sexuality and the female sexual response. It outlines what women should expect from satisfying sexual relationships and what to do about problems they encounter with sexual intimacy.

Part II, The Reproductive System, provides thorough descriptions of both female and male reproductive systems, from early development to mature function. It recommends preventive strategies for maintaining good reproductive health—including essential information about the wealth of contraceptive products available on the market—and covers conditions and illnesses of the female system and how to approach them.

Part III, Sexually Transmitted Diseases, takes a comprehensive look at the currently prevalent diseases transmitted by sexual contact, ranging from seemingly harmless problems such as herpes simplex to the most deadly and fearful diseases such as AIDS. This section gives information about the symptoms of each disease, complications that may arise, various methods of treatment, and most important, how to avoid contracting sexually transmitted diseases.

Part IV, AIDS and Women, discusses the HIV virus responsible for the AIDS epidemic and how it affects women in particular. AIDS is one of the top five leading causes of death among women in the U.S. All women must learn the risk factors of HIV and the available precautions that can help them protect themselves from this fatal disease.

The AMWA Guide to Sexuality provides authoritative information that all women need in today's changing environment. It illuminates health concerns unique to women of the 1990s and offers sound medical advice. Supported by the expertise and experience of the American Medical Women's Association, The AMWA Guide to Sexuality offers a sensitive and sensible approach to helping women lead healthy and sexually fulfilling lives.

CONTENTS

PART I
SEXUALITY
Maj-Britt Rosenbaum, M.D., F.A.P.A., and
Katherine A. O'Hanlan, M.D., F.A.C.O.G., F.A.C.S.

Sexual Development   3
Sexual Response Cycle   4
Sexual Expression   8
Factors that Affect Sexual Function   11
Special Concerns for Women   18
Sexual Problems   23
Therapy   28

PART II
THE REPRODUCTIVE SYSTEM
Katherine A. O'Hanlan, M.D., F.A.C.O.G., F.A.C.S.,
and Jean L. Fourcroy, M.D., PH.D.

Structure and Function   32
Keeping the System Healthy   49
Symptoms   54
Conditions and Disorders in Women   56
Procedures for Women   102
Conditions and Disorders in Men   111
Procedures for Men   120

PART III
SEXUALLY TRANSMITTED DISEASES
Carol Widrow, M.D.

Prevention   127
Types of STDs   130

PART IV
AIDS AND WOMEN
Carol Widrow, M.D.

How HIV Is Transmitted   149
Testing for HIV   155
Prevention of HIV Infection   157
The AIDS Process   162
Treatment for AIDS   169
The Future   170
Editors and Contributors   173
Index   175

The American Medical Women's Association

Guide to Sexuality

PART I
Sexuality

Maj-Britt Rosenbaum, M.D., F.A.P.A.,
and Katherine A. O'Hanlan, M.D.,
F.A.C.O.G., F.A.C.S.

Sexuality is an aspect of an individual's personality that is shaped by biologic, psychological, and social factors. Extending far beyond sexual function, sexuality is a personal set of experiences and values that encompasses a person's sexual identity, her feelings about sexual expression, and how she relates to others sexually. It involves a complex set of interactions that evolve and change throughout a person's life.

Women are increasingly becoming aware of their sexuality and less repressed about their own sexual needs and choices. Because sexuality is highly personal and individualized, there is great variety within a normal range of sexual expression. Women differ in their sexual interest and response, and a woman's feelings about her sexuality may change based on her circumstances and the time of her life. Women's sexual satisfaction often does not occur spontaneously but must be developed. For many women, exploring and learning about sex is a lifelong process. Women should take an active role in this process to ensure that they derive the most enjoyment from it.

Sexuality can be a source of gratification that brings personal contentment, good mental health, and intimacy with a partner. It can also result in anxiety and disappointment when the needs of either or both partners are not met. Sexual problems are common in adults and can be caused by mental and/or physical factors that have a bearing on the delicate and highly subjective balance of what constitutes a satisfying sexual experience. Fortunately, most sexual problems are amenable to treatment.

SEXUAL DEVELOPMENT

The continual process of sexual development begins at the time of conception. It is influenced early in life by identification with a specific gender and is shaped by parents' perceptions, religious values, and cultural aspects. In some cases this can lead to mixed or conflicting messages, which can create confusion in establishing a set of personal values about sex. As a woman matures and discovers her own sexual identity, she can explore methods of expression that are pleasurable and acceptable to her.

A person's biologic sex is established at the time of conception. The genes from the mother and father join to determine whether the baby will be a boy or a girl, and sex organs develop accordingly. At around age 2, a child exhibits characteristics that relate to his or her gender—masculine or feminine. This is the first step in developing a sexual identity.

Gender identity involves an individual's acceptance of his or her biologic sex and demonstration of behavior that can be considered masculine or feminine. There is not always a clear distinction, however, between male and female or masculine and feminine behavior. Usually, in formulating a sexual identity, traits of both sexes are present.

Another aspect of sexual identity is orientation. This relates to whether a person is attracted to the same or the opposite sex. A woman may be attracted to men or to other women or to both. A person's sexual orientation begins to develop during childhood and usually is fixed in the teenage years. Because many cultures provide models only of heterosexuality, however, some lesbians and gay men do not allow themselves honest expression until a few years later.

Physical aspects of sexual development begin to occur during puberty. Changes are triggered by rising levels of hormones and begin between the ages of 9 and 14. Girls begin to develop about 2 years earlier than boys.

During puberty, girls have an increase in height and weight, and their body shape changes to the contours of a woman. First breast buds begin to develop, then armpit and pubic hair sprouts, and then last, menstruation begins. Boys also develop hair on their bodies during puberty. A boy's voice becomes deeper, and his penis and testes grow larger. The new hormones that initiate puberty also create new sexual desires in adolescents.

Both men and women are capable of having full and satisfying sexual function throughout their lives. This cannot always be accomplished without some effort, however. A woman reaches her peak of sexual responsiveness in her late 30s and early 40s, whereas a man reaches his peak in his late teens or early 20s. Women can help ensure their sexual gratification by being aware of what can promote as well as interfere with it. Sexual response follows a natural pattern and anything that interrupts that pattern can create sexual difficulties.

SEXUAL RESPONSE CYCLE

Sexual response follows a cycle that begins with desire, moves through arousal and into plateau, and culminates in orgasm and a return to normal (see "Anatomy of the Sexual Response," page 6). It is not necessary to go through every step of the complete cycle to achieve sexual satisfaction, and women may differ in their experience of sexual response. Sexual response is both emotional and physical. Emotionally, numerous factors can enhance and diminish response. Physically, sexual response follows a pattern that centers around the swelling of the labia and clitoris caused by the congestion of blood and the building of muscle tension throughout the body. The sexual response cycle is not a step-by-step pattern but rather a slow process by which one stage gradually merges into the next.

Desire

Sexual desire precedes and accompanies sexual arousal. It is the excitement of body and mind that makes a person interested in and receptive to sexual stimulation.

Arousal

Sexual arousal begins in women with vaginal lubrication. The amount of lubrication may vary with the amount of stimulation, a woman's previous sexual history, her age, or her hormonal status. Parasympathetic nerves, the "relaxation" nerves, cause the blood vessels serving the genital organs to increase the blood supply and cause congestion. The labia— "lips" surrounding the vulva (the opening to the vagina)—swell from the congestion of blood. The clitoris, a small organ located above the opening to the vagina that is the highly sensitive source of sexual excitement, also swells from congestion. The same congestion is the source of the fluid of sexual excitement, which flows from the vessels into the vagina during sexual stimulation. The nipples of the breasts also may swell and become erect.

As a woman becomes more stimulated, the labia become thicker and redder. The clitoris becomes erect and moves under its hood, or the fold of skin that partly surrounds it. Direct contact of the clitoris may be too intense at this point, but stimulation of the clitoral shaft through the hood can heighten pleasurable sensations.

ANATOMY OF THE SEXUAL RESPONSE

A number of organs play a role in the sexual response cycle:

- *Labia:* Flaps of skin, or "lips," that surround the vulva.

- *Vulva:* The external female genital area and the opening to the internal organs.

- *Vagina:* A canal that leads from the external genital organs to the uterus.

- *Uterus:* A muscular organ found in a woman's pelvic region that holds the fetus during pregnancy.

Plateau

Heart rate, blood pressure, and breathing rates increase as stimulation increases. The vagina expands as the surrounding tissue congests with blood. This is the beginning of the plateau phase, which can last from a few minutes to an hour. Women frequently try to hurry through this essential phase but should, rather, be encouraged to take their time and enjoy it.

Orgasm

The peak of sexual excitement occurs with a series of rhythmic muscle spasms. This pleasurable sensation on the vulva and in the vagina can extend to the uterus and anus and sometimes the whole body. It is a reflex sensation that in women can last 20 to 60 seconds. Orgasm can vary in intensity. Some women can have more than one orgasm, whereas others have one orgasm and find further stimulation of the clitoris to be unappealing. (See Fig. 1.1)

Resolution

After orgasm, breathing, heart rate, and blood pressure return to normal levels. Genital and pelvic organs are no longer engorged with blood and return to their unaroused state. Orgasm is typically followed by a feeling of calmness. Males usually fall into a refractory period, during which they cannot have an erection. A woman does not experience this refractory period, however, and is physically able to achieve multiple orgasms if she is stimulated to do so.

SEXUAL EXPRESSION

Most women feel they must achieve orgasm to be sexually satisfied and that the best way to do this is through direct stimulation of the clitoris. Only about 25 percent of women have orgasm with intercourse according to most surveys of women's sexuality. Women usually need other forms of direct or indirect clitoral stimulation to reach orgasm. This may come in the form of breast stimulation, whole body contact, or most often, by either the woman or her partner directly stimulating the clitoral area.

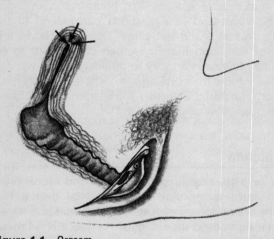

Figure 1.1   Orgasm
During the orgasmic stage, muscular tension is released in contractions that for most women are extremely pleasurable. The arrows show the direction of enlargement of the upper vagina and contractions of the uterus. Orgasm varies greatly in length and intensity for each woman and often feels different at different times for the same woman.

Women must learn what types of stimulation their bodies need during sex so that they can reach an orgasm. Some women learn what brings them pleasure by experimenting with manual masturbation or using sexual devices, such as vibrators. During heterosexual intercourse, certain positions, such as the woman on top or thrusting hip movements, may provide more direct clitoral stimulation. Although some women respond to various forms of stimulation, most show a preference for one form. The usual means of attaining orgasm include (in order of preference) manual or oral stimulation of the clitoris, intercourse with the woman on top, intercourse with the man on top, vibrator stimulation, and the woman stimulating herself to orgasm in front of her partner. For lesbians, the most common method of attaining orgasm is by oral or manual stimulation of the clitoris and vagina.

An adequate level and duration of stimulation is required for a woman to be aroused. Stimulation can be mental as well as physical. Sexual fantasy, combined with physical stimulation, is much more effective than physical stimulation alone.

Most women are biologically able to have an orgasm. If a woman tries too hard, however, she can become the victim of performance anxiety, which inhibits her ability to achieve orgasm. Instead of focusing only on the end result, a woman will find it more satisfying to experience the full range of sexual pleasure that comes with closeness and intimacy. An orgasm is not always essential to having a satisfactory sexual experience.

Most women need a nurturing environment in their relationship to be sexually responsive. Although men desire a nurturing relationship and find their sexual responsiveness enhanced by it, they are not as affected as women are by its absence. The positive emotional tone of a relationship and the resultant feelings of trust and mutual respect are important factors in a woman's sexual expression and response.

Between 5 and 10 percent of women prefer other women as sexual and life partners. Homosexuality has been observed in most animal species and should be regarded as one of the many natural expressions of human sexuality. Sexual orientation appears to be influenced by both the environment and genetics but bears no correlation with any psychological or physiological disease traits. The unfortunate disdain that some cultures have for their homosexual members is without any basis in scientific fact and is a cause for distress among lesbian and gay individuals. Bisexual relationships, when a person has sexual experiences with both men and women, are more common among women than men. Partners in these relationships are often chosen more on the basis of their personal traits rather than their gender.

In some cases, a woman may choose not to have any sexual partners for a given time. She may wish to be celibate for a number of reasons, such as recovering from the loss of a spouse or a broken relationship or wanting to devote attention to another part of her life.

Sexuality and sexual needs are key parts of most people's lives, yet many women are reluctant to talk about them. Understanding personal sexual values is essential to understanding sexual needs, desires, and preferences. These preferences should be communicated to sexual partners so an open attitude toward meeting each other's needs can be maintained.

FACTORS THAT AFFECT SEXUAL FUNCTION

Sexual satisfaction involves a complex interplay of biologic and emotional factors, social conditioning, personal expectations, and physical aspects. It should not be surprising, therefore, that these factors, singly and in combination, can have an impact on sexual function. Stress, performance anxiety, misconceptions about human sexual response, problems in a relationship, a reaction to illness, and specific medical or surgical treatments can lead to sexual difficulties. Some of these influences are temporary, whereas others may require major adjustments or adaptations.

Stress and Anxiety

Stress, emotional problems, fear, and anxiety can interfere with a person's desire to have sex. Daily stresses, such as the demands of children, insufficient time alone with a partner, or the inability to relax, can lead to decreased desire. Concerns about work or finances, family problems, or a personal crisis decrease a person's sexual interest and responsiveness.

Anxiety can often cause sexual problems. It can stem from focusing too much on technique or performance and from evaluating the experience only in terms of performance. Another source of anxiety is concern about the partner's expectations and whether they will be met. This can lead to what is called *spectatoring*, in which a person becomes so absorbed in monitoring what is happening that she is unable to experience it.

One of the most common causes of sexual problems in women is a lack of knowledge about sexuality by their male partners. Men were not born with the specific knowledge or skill to stimulate a woman to orgasm. Most partners need to be taught which methods of stimulation work best for each woman. This can create anxiety when a woman does not know how her body can respond sexually or has a partner who doesn't listen to her. She may also become anxious if her partner wants to perform a sexual act that she is uncomfortable with. Anxiety can also stem from guilt that has its roots in childhood conditioning.

A woman may avoid sex because of fear of pain, of what will happen, of pregnancy, of getting a sexually transmitted disease, or of dealing with issues of unexpressed lesbianism. Other forms of fear are the loss of self and fear of intimacy.

Relationships

Interpersonal relationships with sexual partners can have a strong influence on sexual function and the satisfaction that can be derived from it. An interpersonal problem with a woman's partner is often the cause of a sexual difficulty. It is usually only a matter of time before a problem in a relationship includes a sexual problem. Sometimes the problem in the relationship is caused by a sexual problem. In this case, a woman should communicate her sexual needs to her partner. If the partner doesn't respond or rejects her requests, the problem centers on the relationship and is not sexual.

Sexual problems in relationships often center around communication. A woman may feel shy or embarrassed when talking about sex and may be reluctant to discuss her preferences in case her partner thinks she is criticizing. She also may assume that her partner knows what she wants. This lack of communication goes both ways. It is important for a couple to talk openly about what pleases them as well as what they find troubling.

In the presence of performance anxiety and spectatoring, the partner may feel tension that makes it difficult to talk openly and freely. This often takes the form of not talking about the problem at all, having discussions that lead to angry exchanges, blaming each other, or rationalizing one's behavior. This type of communication often takes nonverbal forms, with partners indicating to each other in various ways their unhappiness in the sexual relationship. Eventually, the couple may cease to have sex and refuse to discuss it.

Couples should try to keep lines of communication open. Partners need to talk to each other and to acknowledge their fears and concerns so they can discuss their sexual problems.

Sexual Abuse

Sexual trauma or abuse as a child can inhibit sexual response in an adult. Some women who have been victims of sexual abuse feel that their sense of trust has been violated and may have difficulty relating to their partners in an intimate and sensual way. Other women respond by completely losing their sexual desire. Another lesser known and rare effect of sexual abuse is relentless sexual seeking and compulsive behavior.

Drugs and Illness

Serious illness is a major personal event that concerns the person who has the illness as well as those around him or her. It often reduces the frequency and quality of sexual activity. Chronic disease can have a negative impact on a woman's ability to feel and be sexual. The effect of illness depends on the disease itself, the age and attitude of the person affected, and the impact on the partner. All serious disease can affect a person's sex life through fatigue, limited energy, and reduced sexual drive. A sexual problem can stem from the disorder or the treatment or both (see "Effects of Drugs on Sexual Function," opposite).

Certain disorders affect sexual activity through damage to nerves that control sexual response. Others are caused by lack of adequate blood circulation. For still others, the cause is not known but can involve a complex interaction of factors, both physical and mental. In many cases, the effects are more obvious in men because they cause impotence. In women, sexual function may be preserved but there may be difficulty with vaginal lubrication. One of the most important aspects of a medical disorder's effect on sexual activity is the amount of pain associated with it. Pain may prevent couples from engaging in sexual activities known to be pleasurable. Although medical disorders can cause physical and psychological problems that may affect sexual adjustment, in many cases interest in sex is not lessened, and patients with such problems can enjoy satisfying sexual experiences (see "Medical Conditions That Can Affect Sexual Function," page 16).

Illness can interfere with sex, just as it interferes

with other activities. For an illness that comes on suddenly and is treated, the effect on sexuality may be temporary. For chronic illness, however, the interference can result in a quality-of-life problem. Women must not hesitate to report changes in sexual

EFFECTS OF DRUGS ON SEXUAL FUNCTION

Medications that interfere with sexual function in women do so by decreasing desire or inhibiting orgasm. The most common of such medications are antihypertensive agents, antipsychotic drugs, and antidepressants. Tamoxifen, a drug used to treat women with breast cancer, can cause vaginal dryness in premenopausal women. Chemotherapy for cancer employs powerful drugs that affect many aspects of a person's bodily function, including sexual drive and ability to become aroused. Similarly, there are numerous drugs that cause sexual problems in men. They include antihypertensive agents, anticonvulsants, tranquilizers and antidepressants, and drugs for treating ulcers and heart disease.

Intoxication with alcoholic beverages diminishes both men's and women's arousal states and inhibits orgasm. Chronic alcohol use also lowers sexual drive. Alcoholics are thus prone to have sexual problems, and these problems are often worsened by concurrent drug abuse. Substance abuse of drugs such as morphine, codeine, and heroin can seriously impair sexual function. Users have lowered sex drive and less sexual activity.

response associated with disease to their doctor. Women should expect to receive help or referral to a knowledgeable therapist; they should be able to pursue a satisfying sex life despite their illness.

Medical Conditions That Can Affect Sexual Function

Arthritis

Painful joints can inhibit sexual activity and the partner may be concerned about causing pain. Arthritis also limits mobility and thus can have an effect on the forms of sexual expression. A woman's membranes may be dry with some forms of arthritis, resulting in a lack of vaginal lubrication. Sexual comfort can be enhanced by using positions that avoid prolonged pressure on affected joints, using vaginal lubricants, and taking pain medication and applying heat to joints before having sex.

Cardiovascular Disease

People with a heart condition may have pain with exercise and lack circulation to the extremities. Although sexual activity may be physically and emotionally stressful, it rarely leads to severe complications in patients with a cardiac disease. The amount of energy expended during normal sexual activity is about the same as climbing a single flight of steps. A person's ability to tolerate exercise can be tested to determine the safety of sexual activity.

Diabetes

Nerve damage, which occurs with diabetes, can lead to women experiencing difficulty having orgasms and impotence in men. In women, this can result in less vaginal lubrication and contraction of the muscles of orgasm. In men, the problem is compounded by lack of blood circulation and hypertension, which also contribute to impotence. Control of diabetes may result in an improvement in sexual function.

Epilepsy

Epilepsy causes an electrical "short circuit" in the messages sent by nerves to the brain. It can result in loss of sex drive, decreased sexual responsiveness, and partial or complete impotence.

Kidney Disease

Complications of kidney disorders can cause loss of sex drive and, in men, impotence. The effects are related to hormone imbalances often associated with this condition as well as nerve damage and other medical problems that are often present. In women, careful attention should be given to possible vaginal infections that could cause discomfort during sexual activity.

Spinal Cord Injury

Any damage to the spinal cord can interfere with sexual function, depending on the location of the injury. It can cause paralysis and loss of sensation, resulting in lack of lubrication in women and impotence in men. Both women and men can often continue to have orgasms, however. With special preparation and devices, women and men with spinal cord injuries can maintain sexual activity.

Stroke

A blockage in the vessels that supply blood to the brain can result in paralysis of part of the body, muscle weakness, and less ability to move around. This can have an effect on sexual activity. Because the nerves are usually not damaged, however, sex is possible with some adjustments.

Thyroid Disease

Any hormone imbalance can affect sexuality. In thyroid disease, changes in hormone levels can cause menstrual problems in women, impotence in men, and loss of sex drive in both. A decrease in energy and other complications can also be a factor. Sexual problems caused by the disease go away when it is treated.

SPECIAL CONCERNS FOR WOMEN

Any change in a woman's life that relates to her reproductive system can raise concerns about her sexuality. These can be normal changes, such as those that come with pregnancy or menopause, or they can be medical problems, such as cancer of the breast or reproductive organs. Having a sexually transmitted disease or an abnormal Pap smear may also cause a woman to experience uneasiness about her sexuality. These conditions can all affect sexual function, especially if the woman is worried about them. A woman should seek advice from her doctor about these conditions and their impact on her sexual life and health.

Pregnancy

There are different patterns of sexual activity during pregnancy. Some women have a decrease in sexual activity during the first three months of pregnancy, an increase in the middle of pregnancy, and a decrease again at the end. In other women, sexual activity decreases steadily during pregnancy, as do sexual interest and the ability to have an orgasm. This variation in activity could be related to a number of factors, including emotional and physical ones. In the beginning of pregnancy, physical discomfort can lead to a decreased desire for sex. In the second trimester, however, women often feel less uncomfortable. Near the end of pregnancy, the discomfort can return. Most women have expressed an increased desire to be held while they are pregnant.

Some couples mistakenly think that making love will hurt the baby, so they avoid having sex. Most women can continue to have sexual relations with their partners all through pregnancy without harming the baby. For the sake of comfort and ease, they may wish to experiment with different positions and techniques that create less pressure on the uterus. If there is a problem in the pregnancy, such as a risk of preterm birth, the doctor may suggest that a couple stop or limit sexual activity.

After pregnancy, women who breast-feed may notice a lack of vaginal lubrication during sexual activity. This is caused by changes in hormone levels and can be relieved with the use of vaginal lubricants or hormones.

Hormone levels return to normal at about 10 weeks after delivery, although there is wide variation among women. Some begin to have menstrual periods as early as 1 month after delivery. Women who breast-feed return to normal more gradually and may not begin having menstrual periods until 36 weeks after delivery. Even though they are not having periods, however, they can become pregnant. Most doctors agree that a woman can begin having sex after pregnancy as soon as she feels comfortable.

Menopause

During menopause, a woman's ovaries stop producing the hormone estrogen. This can lead to changes that affect her sexual function. The main change is vaginal dryness. Lack of vaginal lubrication can make sex painful. Low levels of estrogen may also cause the walls of the vagina to thin and be more prone to sexual discomfort and injury. This can be corrected through estrogen-replacement therapy. The hormone is taken as a pill or absorbed through a patch. Locally applied vaginal cream can also be used.

Women do not lose their sexual drive during or after menopause. Most women continue to enjoy a sexually fulfilling life throughout their later years. Factors that could interfere with this include health and relationship problems, unavailability of partners, and emotional concerns that may accompany menopause.

The nature of a woman's sexual activity may change as she ages. She may take longer to become aroused and may need more stimulation to have an orgasm. Some older women have fewer vaginal contractions during orgasm. Older men may have difficulty getting or keeping an erection. As their sexual needs change with age, couples may move their focus away from the traditional genital-focused approach to other forms of sexual pleasure. These may include manual stimulation, oral-genital stimulation, and rubbing the external genitals against each other. For many couples, although the physical form of their lovemaking may change, the intensity, satisfaction, and frequency remain unchanged.

Older couples who are not comfortable with creating diverse experiences of sexual behavior may find their sexual activity limited. At some point, couples may be content to stop having sex. If both partners are comfortable with this situation, it does not have a negative effect on their relationship.

Sexually Transmitted Disease

Certain diseases are sexually transmitted by both heterosexual activity and possibly also by lesbian sexual activity (see Part III). Herpes causes painful blisters in the genital area. Pelvic inflammatory disease is an infection of the internal pelvic organs that can cause deep vaginal and pelvic pain. Condyloma (venereal warts) are transmitted sexually and can grow to be quite large and uncomfortable. Some sexually transmitted diseases don't cause pain but permanently damage reproductive organs and cause infertility. Sexual activity is the most common way of transmitting the fatal illness AIDS. To avoid contracting a sexually transmitted disease, a woman should practice safe sex: She should always use a condom or rubber dam, with spermicide when she has a sexual relationship with anyone. A woman may elect at some point in the relationship to be monogamous, but there is always some risk from a partner's prior history or possible future infidelity. Furthermore, the partner may be an intravenous drug user, an AIDS risk.

Cancer

Cancer and its treatment can affect a woman's sexuality. In addition to the anxiety produced by the diagnosis, a woman may have concerns about its effect on her future sexual capability. Cancer can also affect a woman's appearance and self-esteem, particularly if it involves loss of an organ. Emotionally, a woman is faced with the possibility of death, disfigurement, and the possible rejection by her partner, and physically, she must confront the rigors of surgery, radiation, or chemotherapy.

Radiation therapy is often used in the treatment of cancer of the cervix, vagina, and uterus. It causes the vagina to lose its elasticity and decrease in size and length. After radiation treatment, a woman may need to use a vaginal dilator coated with estrogen cream to keep her vagina open. It should be used daily, and sexual activity can be resumed as soon as clearance is given by the oncologist.

Surgical treatment of gynecologic cancer may involve hysterectomy, or removal of the uterus. The ovaries and part of the vagina also may be removed. There is some controversy over the role of the uterus in orgasm, but a few women report a difference in the nature of their orgasm after their uterus has been removed. Women who equate the loss of their uterus with the loss of their femininity are more apt to have difficulties postoperatively.

Cancer of the vulva may require removal or reconfiguration of the external genital organs. This will affect appearance and may narrow the opening to the vagina. Conservative surgery that retains near- ly normal appearance and function has cure rates similar to radical surgery and is used in most cases.

Colorectal cancer is the third leading cause of death from cancer in the United States. If the rectum and part of the colon are removed surgically, the nerves in the area may be damaged and affect sexual response. The presence of a colostomy (an opening in the abdominal wall to drain the colon after the rec- tum is removed) may inhibit sexual activity initially.

Breast cancer, and in particular mastectomy, can have a major psychological effect on a woman as well as on her partner. The woman may feel deformed or mutilated, resulting in low self-esteem and an inability to function sexually. She may also experi- ence rejection by her partner.

About 33 percent of women who have had mas- tectomies have not resumed sexual activity 6 months after discharge from the hospital. This may be related to factors in the woman or her partner or both. Counseling a woman and her partner in advance of surgery may help them cope better. Group therapy for the cancer survivor and the spouse and family can help restore and maintain the relationships and may have beneficial effects on survival probability.

SEXUAL PROBLEMS

Sexual problems can arise at any stage of the sexual response cycle. They can occur at any time in a woman's life, and they can appear after a woman has enjoyed a long-term satisfying relationship. Sexual problems can occur in four basic areas: lack of desire, lack of arousal, lack of orgasm, and pain during intercourse.

Lack of Desire

Some women lack interest in sex. They may avoid initiating sex or participating in it and be slow or unable to achieve arousal. If they do have sex, they often do not find it very satisfying.

Lack of desire is most often caused by a problem in the couple's relationship. There may be feelings of anger or resentment, which may stem from previous sexual failures or from other problems in the relationship, such as conflicts in attitudes or values. A woman who has difficulty having an orgasm may become conditioned to failure, eventually losing her ability to become aroused and then losing her desire to have sex.

Lack of desire can also be affected by all of the other factors that influence sexual response. It can occur in response to a temporary situation, such as stress or illness, or it can develop into a long-term problem. It can also have a physical basis, such as a reaction to drugs, but it more often results from an emotional response to anxiety, depression, and guilt. Lack of desire for members of the opposite sex can occur at any age if a woman begins dealing with repressed awareness of her lesbianism.

Counseling can be effective in treating sexual problems involving low desire or a lack of desire. These problems are more complex and difficult to treat than other sexual problems, and psychotherapy is often needed to help the woman explore the underlying conflict.

Lack of Arousal

Some women have an interest in sex but are unable to become aroused. Such women may have difficulty achieving adequate vaginal lubrication for intercourse. This is often the result of a lack of stimulation. The woman and her partner may not know how to help her become aroused. Frequently, lack of arousal is related to lack of holding, kissing, and caressing or may be caused by a lack of technical skills. The woman may feel uncomfortable communicating her likes and dislikes to her partner. Her partner may not understand or be able to follow her instructions. Exercises have been developed to help couples overcome this problem (see "Therapy," page 28). They are designed to teach individuals how to better relate to their partners physically and how to minimize performance pressure or anxiety.

Lack of arousal also may occur if a woman is having feelings of fear, anger, or guilt about sex. These feelings can arise from negative or constricting messages about sex as a child. Such lessons need to be unlearned as an adult.

Lack of Orgasm

As many as 20 percent of women have never had or rarely ever have an orgasm with sexual activity. Surveys show that only about 45 percent of heterosexual women but 95 percent of lesbians have orgasms regularly. Almost all women are physiologically capable of having an orgasm, either through self-stimulation or partner stimulation—manually, orally, or with a vibrator. Most heterosexual women require some form of direct clitoral stimulation in addition to intercourse to have an orgasm. It is possible that orgasms are more frequent among lesbians because their most frequent form of sexual activity involves direct clitoral stimulation.

Some women don't have an orgasm because they have not been adequately aroused. Orgasm cannot occur without a high level of arousal, something some women may fail to recognize. They may feel that heterosexual intercourse is the only "acceptable" way to be stimulated and refuse other forms of more direct stimulation, possibly cutting short arousal.

A woman may try so hard to achieve an orgasm that she becomes a spectator rather than a participant. She may be so eager and so anxious to have an orgasm that her body becomes too tense and is unable to respond.

In general, problems that cause lack of orgasm are the same as those that cause other sexual problems. Treatment focuses on exercises to learn how the female body responds and on how to provide adequate stimulation. It can also involve learning new approaches to sexual expression.

Pain During Intercourse

Two conditions, called *dyspareunia* and *vaginismus*, are characterized by pain during vaginal penetration. They can be caused by a physical or emotional factor or a combination of both.

Dyspareunia may involve pain with initial vaginal penetration, with deep thrusting, or following sexual activity. It can occur if there is a lack of estrogen to allow vaginal lubrication, with a pelvic infection, in the presence of a tumor or cyst, or with a condition called endometriosis (in which cells similar to the lining of the uterus grow outside the uterus and cause inflammation).

Vaginismus is a spasm of the pubic muscles of the lower vagina that makes penetration by the penis or by any object into the vagina painful, difficult, or at times impossible. Some women are unable to even have a gynecologic examination, whereas others experience vaginismus only during sex.

Vaginismus may be related to a previous painful experience such as childhood sexual abuse or rape as an adult. It can be caused by a number of medical conditions, such as infections, vaginal irritations, or pelvic or anal skin problems. It can also be a response to fear.

With dyspareunia, once the cause of the symptoms is treated, the problem usually goes away. With vaginismus, some form of psychotherapy is essential. It may be necessary for a woman to perform exercises with either her finger or a dilator to condition herself to the sensation of something being inserted into her vagina.

Male Sexual Dysfunction

Impotence is the common term for male inability to achieve the arousal state and to maintain an erection. Other forms of male sexual dysfunction include premature or retarded ejaculation and lack of sexual desire.

Because of the differences in their sexual development, men and women of the same age often differ in their sexual interest and responsiveness. As a natural part of aging, an older man's erection is not as strong and it doesn't last as long. Erectile dysfunction can also be caused by alcohol and drug abuse, medications, medical conditions, and surgery.

Emotional factors such as stress, depression, fear, and hostility often contribute to male sexual dysfunction. For example, men often experience impotence after divorce or death of a spouse.

If the impotence occurs suddenly and reappears off and on, it is usually considered psychological in nature. If it appears gradually and becomes progressively worse, it is likely to have a physical cause. If a man has firm erections while asleep at night he is usually physically able to have an erection during intercourse. The cause of the problem then tends to be psychological.

Erectile dysfunction that has a psychological basis is treated through counseling. If the cause is physical, the choices involve creating other satisfying methods of sexual expression, having a device surgically implanted to enlarge the penis to its erect size, or giving up sex.

If a man cannot have an erection, he cannot have vaginal intercourse, although other forms of sexual expression may be just as satisfying. If treatment or removal of the agent that is causing impotence doesn't work, a couple may use other forms of manual-oral stimulation. A man can have an orgasm without having an erection.

THERAPY

If a woman or her partner has a problem that cannot be resolved through communication and exploring new ways of expressing sexuality, the couple may find it helpful to seek professional advice and counseling. Most therapists view sexual problems as relating to couples, not individuals. Treatment involves a series of steps in behavior modification aimed at reducing the demand for performance, identifying and modifying emotions that interfere with sexual responses, and teaching the couple physical and emotional behaviors that promote responsiveness.

Sex therapy is based on the principle that sexual problems are learned behavior patterns. Therapists help the couple identify barriers to sexual responsiveness that may arise from learned behavior such as lack of knowledge, guilt, fear, and cultural attitudes. The therapist then helps the couple remove these barriers through a process of relearning. The couple also explores aspects of their relationship that may be causing sexual problems.

Sex therapy often includes exercises called sensate focus. These exercises help the couple relate to each other physically without performance pressure or anxiety. Each partner takes turns caressing the other's body, slowly progressing to genital stimulation then, if desired, to sexual activity. Sensate focus is designed to help couples develop nonverbal means of communicating to each other how they like to be stimulated.

A woman who suffers from lack of arousal may benefit from a series of self-stimulation exercises designed to help her become more acquainted with her body and with what stimulates her sexually. It involves a step-by-step approach to manual stimulation to orgasm by the woman herself, then in front of her partner, then with her partner.

Sex therapists can come from different fields and levels of education. In seeking a qualified one, the following criteria should be met:

- Advanced degree in the profession: M.D. (psychiatrist), Ph.D. (psychologist), M.S.W. (social worker), M.A. or M.S. (marital and family therapist or nurse), or M.F.C. (marriage and family counselor).

- Competence in working with couples with marital problems.

- Training in human sexuality and the treatment of sexual dysfunction.

- Certification by the American Association of Sex Educators, Counselors, and Therapists (AASECT).

Sources of information on sex therapists include clinics sponsored by a university, medical school, or social agency. A university department of psychology or medical school department of psychiatry may also be able to provide a referral. Do not accept referrals from a doctor, clergymember, family member, or friend without thoroughly checking the credentials of the therapist and asking about his or her qualifications.

Most people will have a transient sexual problem at some point in their lives. This is certainly normal. Sexuality is an important part of living, and it should be experienced to its fullest potential. That can be achieved through self-awareness, communication, and professional support as needed.

PART II

The Reproductive System

Katherine A. O'Hanlan, M.D.,
F.A.C.O.G., F.A.C.S.,
and Jean L. Fourcroy, M.D., PH.D.

The organs that form the reproductive system allow humans to reproduce. Men and women have different reproductive systems that work in unison to create new life. If something goes awry with the components of the female or male reproductive system, it can affect not only the ability to have children but may also cause serious disorders warranting early detection and treatment.

STRUCTURE AND FUNCTION

The reproductive and genital organs of a fetus form during the fourth week of pregnancy. At that time, nerve, blood vessel, and tissue bundles form in patterns that distinguish males from females when they are fully developed. Development of these organs in the fetus ends during the first trimester. (See Fig. 2.1)

Many of the anatomic structures in one sex correspond to those in the other. For instance, the female clitoris and the male penis are derived from the same structures, contain the same number of nerves, and are the site of intense sensitivity during sexual activity.

A child is born with male or female reproductive organs, but these organs remain undeveloped until puberty. Then a spurt of hormones causes rapid growth and development of reproductive organs, changing body structure and function and making a person capable of reproduction.

Females usually mature sexually between the ages of 10 and 14, when the ovaries begin producing the hormone estrogen. This causes the hips to widen, breasts to develop, and body hair to grow. It also triggers menstruation, the monthly cycle of bleeding that is a key part of a woman's fertility. Women continue to produce estrogen and menstruate until about age 50. The amount of estrogen produced by her ovaries slowly decreases until a woman reaches menopause, when her periods stop and she is no longer able to become pregnant naturally.

Males develop sexually a little later than females. At puberty, the hormone testosterone causes an increase in height, muscle development, and the growth of the sex organs, which then produce sperm. Boys may have nocturnal emissions of semen, or wet dreams, at puberty. Around age 50, the production of testosterone in men may decrease. Although lowered levels of testosterone do not seem to affect the ability to have an erection, it may result in a decrease in sexual desire.

The Female Reproductive System

A woman's external genital area is called the vulva. It is made up of the labia minora—the inner lips enclosing the opening to the vagina—and the labia majora—the outer, hair-bearing lips surrounding the opening of the vagina and the urethra, the opening to the bladder. The clitoris is a small bud-shaped organ, located just above the urethra. It is the most sensitive area of the external female genitals. Bartholin's glands are located on either side of the vaginal opening.

The vagina is a muscular tube leading from the external genital organs to the uterus. The opening of the uterus, the cervix, projects into the upper end of the vagina. (See Fig. 2.2) It varies in shape and size

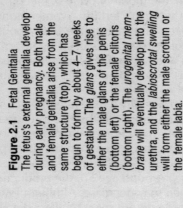

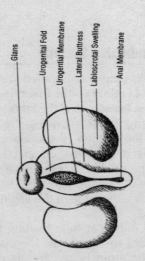

Glans

Urogenital Fold

Urogenital Membrane

Lateral Buttress

Labioscrotal Swelling

Anal Membrane

Figure 2.1 Fetal Genitalia
The fetus's external genitalia develop during early pregnancy. Both male and female genitalia arise from the same structure (top), which has begun to form by about 4–7 weeks of gestation. The *glans* gives rise to either the male glans of the penis (bottom left) or the female clitoris (bottom right). The *urogenital membrane* will eventually develop into the urethra, and the *labioscrotal swelling* will form either the male scrotum or the female labia.

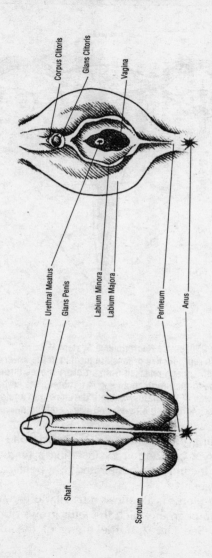

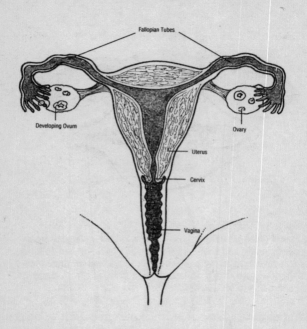

Figure 2.2   Female Reproductive System
A woman's reproductive organs are located in the lower abdomen.
Each month, an egg released from an *ovary* moves through a *fallopian tube* to the *uterus*. If an egg is fertilized, it is embedded in
the inner wall of the uterus, where it develops into a fetus. The
fetus passes through the *cervix* and *vagina* during delivery.

depending on whether a woman has had children.
The cervix can be felt by inserting a finger into the
vagina. It cannot be penetrated by a penis, a tampon,
or a finger.

The uterus is a hollow, muscular organ, about the
size of a pear, in which the fetus grows during pregnancy. (See Fig. 2.3) The lining of the uterus, the

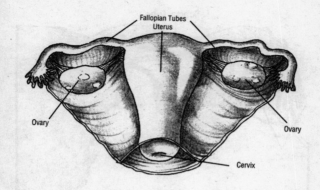

Figure 2.3   The Uterus
The uterus (seen here from the back) is a hollow, muscular organ that varies in size and shape. In women who have not had children, it usually measures about two and a half to a little over three inches long. In women who have had children, it ranges from about three and a half to four inches long.

endometrium, changes in thickness depending on a woman's menstrual cycle. The fallopian tubes extend from either side of the upper end of the uterus. They are about 4 inches in length and reach outward toward the ovaries. (See Fig. 2.4) The ovaries are the female sex organs that produce eggs and female hormones.

A woman is born with 2 million undeveloped eggs in her ovaries—more than enough to last during her reproductive life. Each month, an egg matures in the ovaries and is released into the fallopian tubes. This process is called ovulation. If a man and a woman have sex at that time and the man's sperm unites with the woman's egg, fertilization occurs. The fertilized egg then moves into the

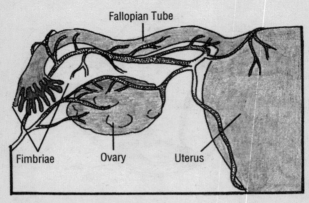

Figure 2.4 The Fallopian Tubes
The fallopian tubes extend outward from either side of the uterus.
At the end of each tube, fingerlike projections called *fimbriae* are
situated close to the surface of the ovary. During ovulation, the egg
released by one of the ovaries enters the tube through the fimbriae.

woman's uterus where it becomes attached to
the endometrium and begins to grow into a fetus.
(See Fig. 2.5) If the egg is not fertilized, it dissolves
in her body. The endometrium, which thickens
before ovulation to prepare for the fertilized egg,
begins to break down and menstruation, or bleeding
occurs. The hormones estrogen and progesterone,
produced in the ovaries, regulate the menstrual
cycle (see "Hormones of the Reproductive System,"
page 40).

Estrogen is secreted by the ovaries throughout
a woman's reproductive years, affecting all the cells
of the body. Special estrogen receptors are located in
the breasts, the lining of the uterus, the cervix, and
the upper vagina. Cells with estrogen receptors grow
when estrogen is in the blood, whether it is secreted

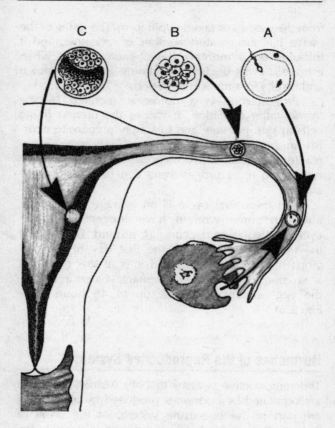

Figure 2.5 Fertilization
The process of fertilization begins with the release of an egg from
one of the ovaries. Normally, penetration of an egg by a sperm
occurs in the far end of a fallopian tube (A) anywhere from 12 to
24 hours after ovulation. By the time the fertilized egg has reached
the near end of the tube (B), it has already begun to divide.
Implantation in the wall of the uterus (C) usually occurs 3–4 days
after ovulation.

from the ovaries or taken in pill form. The lining of the uterus has the greatest number of receptors, and it thickens on a monthly basis. Each month, when estrogen levels decline, the lining is broken down and results in a menstrual period.

Progesterone is a hormone secreted by the ovaries after ovulation. It causes the uterine lining cells to stop growing and to simply prepare to nourish an egg should it be fertilized and become implanted in the uterus. At menopause, when ovulation ceases, no more progesterone can be made by the ovaries.

The menstrual cycle is an average of 28 days, although some women have longer or shorter cycles. Ovulation occurs at around day 14 of the cycle (counting from the first day of the previous menstrual period), and it is at this time that a woman can become pregnant. Once released, the egg remains fertile for up to 48 hours. (See Fig. 2.6)

Hormones of the Reproductive System

The reproductive systems of both women and men are regulated by hormones produced by glands that are part of the endocrine system. At the onset of puberty, the hypothalamus gland sends a signal to the pituitary gland to secrete hormones that cause the development of sexual organs.

The hypothalamus cells in the brain secrete peptides to signal the pituitary. This area regulates eating, drinking, sleeping, waking, body temperature, chemical balances, heart rate, hormones, sex, and emotions.

The pituitary, a small, gray, rounded gland attached to the base of the brain, is an endocrine gland secreting a number of hormones. The pituitary is often referred to as the master gland of the body.

Gonads (sex glands) are the testes in the male and the ovaries in the female. These glands produce the male and female hormones that regulate reproduction:

- Estrogen is the female hormone produced by the ovaries that is responsible for ovulation.

- Progesterone is a female hormone produced by the ovaries after ovulation. It triggers the men-

---

ANABOLIC STEROIDS

Androgens are male sex hormones, one of which is testosterone. Anabolic steroids are synthetic androgens that have been designed to enhance the growth-promoting effects of androgens. Anabolic steriods are occasionally used, under a doctor's supervision, to treat skeletal and growth disorders and certain types of anemia. Steroids are also used illegally, mainly by athletes who want to quickly build muscle tissue. They have many potentially serious side effects: reduced sperm production, decreased size of the testes, and reduced natural sex hormone production, resulting in a diminished sex drive. Steroids can also lead to liver damage and cardiovascular disease and, if taken in early puberty, result in short stature.

strual period. It prepares the uterine lining for the fertilized egg.

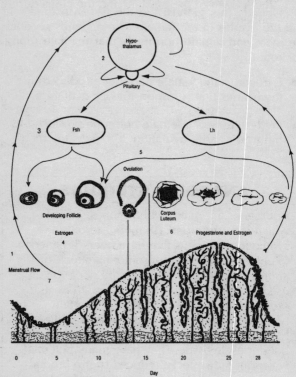

Figure 2.6 The Menstrual Cycle
During the menstrual cycle, an egg is produced, released into a fallopian tube, and eventually, the uterine lining is shed if fertilization does not occur. The average menstrual cycle typically lasts 28 days, but it may vary from 23 to 35 days.

■ Testosterone is the gonadal steroid secreted by the male. After puberty, the normal male secretes testosterone daily. It is responsible for the growth of the prostate and the penis during puberty.

1. The cycle begins on day 1 of menstruation, when the lining of the uterus (the *endometrium*) is shed as menstrual blood. Menstruation occurs in response to a decline in the hormones estrogen and progesterone, which occurs when an egg is not fertilized.

2. The decrease in estrogen and progesterone causes the *hypothalamus* to send a message to the *pituitary*.

3. The pituitary in turn releases *follicle-stimulating hormone* (FSH). Follicles are the structures inside the ovaries that produce eggs for fertilization. Each month, one follicle will produce the egg for that cycle.

4. FSH continues to be produced during days 1–13 of the menstrual cycle. Under its influence, the developing follicle begins to produce estrogen. This hormone stimulates the endometrium to grow and thicken in preparation for a fertilized egg. At this time, the mucus normally produced by the cervix becomes thin, clear, and watery.

5. As the developing follicle continues to produce estrogen, the hormone triggers the pituitary to release *luteinizing hormone* (LH). LH stimulates the follicle to release an egg into a fallopian tube. This event, called *ovulation*, typically occurs on day 14 of the cycle.

6. After releasing the egg, the follicle begins to change into a structure known as the *corpus luteum*. This structure then begins to produce the hormone progesterone, which causes the lining of the uterus to continue to thicken in preparation for a fertilized egg.

7. If the egg is not fertilized, a sharp drop occurs in the production of estrogen and progesterone. This triggers the shedding of the endometrium, which marks the start of another menstrual cycle.

The Male Reproductive System

Like that of females, the reproductive system of males is regulated by hormones, which have an effect through birth, puberty, maturity, and aging (see "Hormones of the Reproductive System"). The male genital organs (testes) produce sperm cells and transport them through a series of ducts to the female reproductive system. (See Fig. 2.7)

Each day a male produces about 50 million sperm, the smallest living cells of the body. When a man ejaculates during sexual intercourse, he releases millions of sperm, but only one joins with a woman's egg to fertilize it. Sperm cells can live up to 5 days inside a woman. If a sperm cell joins with a woman's egg released at ovulation, fertilization occurs and a woman becomes pregnant.

The penis, a rod-shaped organ, also transports urine (see Fig. 2.8). Within the penis is the urethra, which carries the urine from the bladder. The penis also holds many blood vessels, which become engorged with blood during sexual excitement, causing an erection (tumescence).

The testes are two egg-shaped organs contained in a pouch of skin called the scrotum that hangs behind the penis. In each of the testicles there is a tightly packed mass of tubes surrounded by a protective capsule. Leydig cells in the testes produce the hormone testosterone, and the tubes in the testes produce sperm. The production of sperm requires a temperature that is lower than the body's internal temperature. Spermatic cords suspend the testicles within the scrotum and help to maintain the correct temperature for sperm production. When the outside temperature is low, the cords draw the testicles upward, nearer to the warm body.

The epididymis is a cordlike structure beside and behind the testes that transports sperm cells from the testicles to the seminal vesicles. Lying behind the bladder, the seminal vesicles store sperm. The sperm are mingled in a fluid that forms part of the semen that is released during ejaculation.

The vas deferens is a thick muscular tube, which is about 1/4 inch in diameter and about 18 inches long. It assists in the transportation and propulsion of sperm and fluid from the testicle in ejaculation. Vasectomy is a method of male sterilization by blocking or cutting the vas deferens.

The prostate is a walnut-shaped gland located below the bladder, surrounding the urethra. Its main function is to produce a fluid that nourishes sperm and helps transport sperm through the urethra during ejaculation.

Cowper's glands, also known as bulbourethral glands, are two teardrop-shaped structures each the size of a pea. They are situated on either side of the urethra and provide mucus and chemicals during sexual excitement. The mucus washes the urethra in preparation for ejaculation and serves as a lubricant.

Semen is the fluid that is ejaculated during the male sexual act. An ejaculation may contain as many as 120 million sperm (see Fig. 2.9). Semen is milky white fluid containing not only sperm but also secretions from the seminal vesicles, prostate gland, and bulbourethral glands. These fluids combine to create the best possible conditions for the survival and function of the sperm. The mucus furnishes lubrication, but initially makes the sperm somewhat immobile. Within about a half hour after ejaculation, however, the fluid dissolves the mucus and the sperm become highly mobile.

Erection of the penis is provoked by sexual stimulation. Impulses are transmitted from the brain down the spinal cord to the penis by parasympathetic nerves. The messages signal the corpora cavernosa,

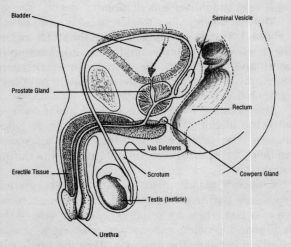

Figure 2.7 The Male Reproductive System
Sperm cells are produced in the *testes*, two roundish organs located within the *scrotum*. To develop normally, sperm cells need a temperature that is slightly lower (about 95°F) than normal body temperature. The scrotum's location outside the warmer body cavity provides the right conditions for sperm production. After being stored in the *epididymis*, a structure lying next to the testes, sperm cells move through the *vas deferens* and enter the *urethra*. There they are bathed in secretions from the *prostate gland* and the *seminal vesicles*, from which semen is formed. With sexual stimulation, secretions from the *Cowper's glands* help to lubricate the inside of the urethra, and the penis becomes erect. During ejaculation, the sperm-containing semen passes through the urethra to the outside of the body. Shown here is a penis with the *foreskin*, a sheath of tissue covering the head (*glans*) of the penis, intact; in many males, the foreskin is removed shortly after birth.

two rod-shaped bundles of muscle in the penis on either side, to relax and fill with blood. As they fill, the corpora cavernosa expand and press against the veins that would normally drain blood from the penis. The penis becomes firm and erect, allowing penetration into the female vagina during sexual intercourse.

Sensations on the skin of the penis that occur during intercourse stimulate the organ's numerous nerve endings. These impulses are carried back to the

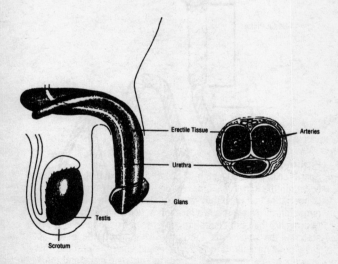

Figure 2.8 Internal Anatomy of the Penis
The shaft of the penis consists of spongy erectile tissue, through which two large arteries and the urethra run lengthwise. During sexual arousal, blood flow through these arteries increases, and the small veins that normally drain the tissue are temporarily pressed shut. Blood cannot drain, and the penis becomes enlarged and rigid.

brain. The sexual stimulation gradually builds in intensity until it causes a reflex action. Impulses travel down the nerves, passing through the genital organs, and trigger ejaculation, the rhythmic contractions of the smooth muscle of the testicles, which

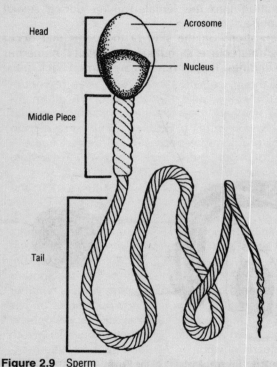

Figure 2.9 Sperm
The head, or *nucleus*, of a sperm cell contains 23 chromosomes. At the tip is the *acrosome*, which contains enzymes that break down barriers surrounding the female ovum. The *middle piece* consists of structures that power cell movement. The rapid movements of the *tail* propel the sperm cell through the female reproductive tract.

expel their contents, the semen, into the urethra. The bulbourethral glands discharge additional amounts of mucus at this time. The act of ejaculation, and the feelings of intense pleasure associated with it, are the male orgasm or climax.

KEEPING THE SYSTEM HEALTHY

Understanding and monitoring your own reproductive system is key to keeping it healthy. Health maintenance involves routine self-examinations, regular checkups, prevention of problems, and being alert to signs of problems so they can be treated early. A number of practitioners treat the reproductive system (see "Health Care Practitioners," page 121).

The reproductive systems of both women and men are vulnerable to sexually transmitted diseases (STDs), such as syphilis, gonorrhea, herpes, chlamydia, human papillomavirus (HPV), and AIDS. To protect against STDs, you should limit your number of sexual partners and always use a condom during sexual intercourse. A woman having sex with another woman should be careful not to have contact with her partner's genital fluids or with any open sores on her partner's body. (The use of a dental dam or cellophane wrap has been advocated but has not been shown to be as clearly of value as the condom is for heterosexuals.) In men, certain STDs can appear as an inflammation of the urethra or a discharge, but also can occur without symptoms. In women, there may be no symptoms. Both women and men should be alert to the early signs of STDs, get treatment immediately, and avoid spreading the disease to others (see Part III).

For Women

Every woman's genitals are shaped individually, with different sizes for inner lips, outer lips, and clitoris. Women of all ages should be familiar with the appearance of their genitals and be aware of what is normal for them. In this way, changes that may be the only signs of certain infections or precancerous conditions can be detected early. Early diagnosis means conditions can be treated before they have advanced to later stages. Small sores, ulcers, raw areas, or pigmented areas can be the first and earliest signs of cancer of the vulva. Use a mirror to inspect your vulva monthly to look for these signs.

Women should protect themselves from unwanted pregnancy by using some method of birth control. Ideally, the birth control method should also protect against infections; a barrier method, such as a condom, is ideal. Of course no method is perfect, and failures of contraception do occur. Early diagnosis of a missed period allows you maximum choice in expression of your reproductive desires. If you have had sex without birth control or your birth control has failed, ask your doctor about postcoital, or emergency, contraception.

You should have a pelvic examination and a Pap test annually to detect changes in the cervix that could be early signs of cancer (see "The Pap Test," opposite, and Fig. 2.10). Depending on your situation, your doctor may suggest you have this done more or less often. Any unusual bleeding, pain, or discharge should be brought to the attention of a doctor.

The Pap Test

The Pap test was named after Dr. George Papanicolaou, the physician who developed it. A Pap test can detect changes in the cells on the cervix that could be early signs of cancer. For the test, a woman lies on an examining table with her feet in stirrups. An instrument called a speculum is inserted into her vagina to hold it open. With a small brush or scraper, a sample of cells is removed from the cervix and placed on a glass slide so it can be studied under a microscope.

If menstruation starts and is heavy at the time of an appointment, the appointment should be rescheduled. Also, a woman should not douche before the test.

Test results are reported in categories according to the Bethesda System. A negative result means that there are no abnormal cells present in the sample of cells. A positive result means that some abnormal cells are present and may require further testing. As with any test, however, the results depend on the quality of the lab work and the person evaluating the cells.

The Pap test has greatly reduced the number of deaths from cancer of the cervix, and is used to prevent cervical cancer. The test should be performed annually, with a pelvic exam, for women who have been sexually active or who have reached the age of 18. If results are normal for three consecutive years, the woman is in a monogamous relationship or is celibate, and has no risk factors such as infection with human papillomavirus or smoking, she may then have a Pap test every three years. Many physicians feel that a yearly Pap test will better detect abnormal cells that can develop into cancer.

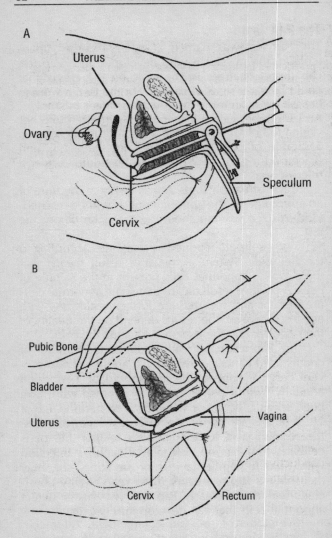

A

Uterus

Ovary

Speculum

Cervix

B

Pubic Bone

Bladder

Uterus

Vagina

Cervix

Rectum

Figure 2.10 Tests
A woman should have a gynecologic exam, including a Pap smear, at least once a year or more if her doctor advises it. The Pap test (A) is performed by inserting an instrument called a *speculum* into the vagina to hold the walls of the vagina apart. A small spatula or brush is then used to collect a sample of cells from the cervix. The cell sample is then smeared onto a glass slide, which is examined under a microscope. A biannual pelvic exam (B) is recommended for every woman. For this exam, the doctor feels the shape, size, and position of the internal reproductive organs by inserting two fingers into the vagina and pressing down on the abdomen with the other hand. Many doctors also perform a rectal exam afterward.

For Men

Recognition and treatment of problems that can arise in the reproductive system as a man ages are essential for a healthy life. Men should have regular checkups to watch for early signs of problems. For example, signs of prostate enlargement include changes or problems with urination such as more frequent urination, a feeling of a need to urinate, and a weak stream of urine. The checkup should include a thorough history and a physical examination. The history should include a family history as well as an occupational and medical history, past genitourinary surgery, or trauma to the reproductive organs. Men should ask their doctors questions regarding any illnesses, changes in sex drive, or drugs that may interfere with reproductive health.

Prostate gland enlargement does not increase the risk of prostate cancer, but cancer could be present at the same time or develop later. Many older men have some symptoms of prostate enlargement. All men over age 50 should have digital rectal examinations once a year to detect prostate cancer. The digital rectal exam involves the insertion of a finger into the rectum to feel the prostate. This important part of total health care can detect enlargement, abnormal texture, or hard areas of the prostate that could be signs of cancer.

Men of all ages should perform testicular self-examination monthly to detect problems that could be a sign of cancer of the testes. It only takes a few minutes and can be done easily and painlessly, preferably after a warm bath or shower or in a warm room when the scrotum is relaxed. To perform the exam, roll each testicle between the thumbs and forefingers of both hands. Any hard lumps or nodules should be brought to the attention of a physician.

SYMPTOMS

Any signs or symptoms of problems in the reproductive system warrant medical attention. In women, problems that can signal a disorder include abnormal bleeding or discharge, pain, or a change in the appearance of the genital organs. In men, changes in their urination or pain can signal prostate enlargement or cancer. In both women and men, any unusual lump or growth that can be felt or seen should receive medical attention.

In Women

In young women, any irregular bleeding may be linked to problems with the hormones secreted by the ovaries. In older women, changes in their menstrual periods could signal menopause. Some women may have irregular, unpredictable, and sometimes heavy bleeding during menopause. They have a slightly higher chance of developing precancerous or cancerous changes of the endometrium and should be monitored by a physician. An endometrial biopsy can determine whether precancerous changes are taking place. In this technique, a sample of the tissue lining the uterus is obtained and studied. After menopause, when a woman has stopped having menstrual periods for 12 months, any bleeding should be evaluated.

It is normal for women to have a clear vaginal discharge. This discharge cleans the vagina, maintains its normal state, and keeps it free of organisms. A discharge that is white or yellow, thick or frothy, or has an odor could be a sign of an infection. Itching also may occur. These symptoms could signal a major or minor problem; have them checked so the cause can be identified and treated.

Pain in the pelvic area can occur for many reasons, although it is usually due to either a cramping of the uterus or conditions affecting the ovaries. Pain in the pelvic region also can be related to any of the anatomic structures in this area, including the ureters, bladder, and rectum. If the pain is sudden, severe, and long lasting, or interferes with daily activities, consult your physician.

A pain in your right or left side can be a sign of ovulation. This pain, called *mittelschmerz* (literally, middle pain), is caused by the release of the egg. It may be accompanied by a clear vaginal discharge and increased sex drive. On rare occasions, there may be slight bleeding.

In Men

Certain symptoms can signal problems with the prostate in men. Many older men have enlarged prostate glands, but this condition does not lead to cancer. Prostate cancer is common in older men, however, so it should be considered when symptoms such as the following are present:

- Hesitant, interrupted, or weak stream of urine
- A sense of urgency, leaking, or dribbling of urine
- More frequent need to urinate, especially at night
- Difficulty starting or holding back urination
- Inability to urinate
- Weak flow of urine
- Painful urination or bloody urine
- Painful ejaculation
- Pain in the lower back, hips, upper thighs

Any of these symptoms requires further evaluation by a primary care physician or, if necessary, a urologist.

CONDITIONS AND DISORDERS IN WOMEN

The female reproductive system is a fairly complicated mechanism that sustains the monthly cycles that are part of fertility as well as pregnancy and childbirth. Because of the complexity of the reproductive organs and the functions needed to maintain them, some normal conditions as well as disorders may require regular medical attention.

Birth Control

Many methods of birth control, or contraception, are available that have a very high degree of safety and effectiveness (see "Contraceptive Failure Rates," page 58). These methods allow you to choose if and when you wish to have children and to plan your family just as you plan other aspects of your life. Without such methods, up to 85 percent of sexually active women using no contraception would be expected to become pregnant in a year. Some methods, such as condoms and spermicides, also provide protection against STDs and cancer of the cervix. All of them allow you control over your reproduction (see "Women's Choices About Contraception," page 59).

Hormonal Methods

Pregnancy can be prevented by using hormones to regulate fertility. The hormone estrogen prevents ovulation, the release of an egg. The hormone progesterone blocks the release of the egg during ovulation, although not as well as estrogen, and creates an environment in the uterine lining that makes pregnancy unlikely. These hormones may be used alone or in combination, depending on the technique.

Hormones are used for postcoital, or emergency, contraception, also known as the morning-after pill. A doctor or family planning clinic can prescribe the pill, which is usually a combination of birth control

CONTRACEPTIVE FAILURE RATES*

Method	Percentage of Average Use†
Contraceptive implants	0.05%
Vasectomy	0.2
Contraceptive injections	0.4
Tubal sterilization	0.5
IUD	4.0
Pill	6.0
Condom (male)‡	16.0
Cervical cap	18.0
Diaphragm	18.0
Periodic abstinence	19.0
Sponge	24.0
Withdrawal	24.0
Condom (female)‡	26.0
Spermicides	30.0
No method (chance)	85.0

*The failure rate is the estimated percentage of all women using the method who will have an unplanned pregnancy in the first year of use.

†Using a method consistently and correctly—the right way, all the time—makes birth control more effective than these rates show.

‡These methods are most effective against sexually transmitted diseases.

WOMEN'S CHOICES ABOUT CONTRACEPTION

A woman's choice about which method of birth control to use is largely affected by whether she wishes to have children in the future. Women who do wish to have children choose oral contraceptives most often (49 percent), whereas those who do not plan to have children or who have completed their families choose sterilization (61 percent). About 10 percent of women do not use any form of birth control. These women account for approximately 53 percent of all unintended pregnancies in the United States, half of which end in abortion. Women who are sexually active and not planning to become pregnant should exercise their options of birth control to avoid unintended pregnancy.

Among all women, these are the percentages of women who select specific methods:

Oral contraceptives	27.7%
Tubal sterilization	24.8
Condom	13.1
Periodic abstinence	2.1
IUD	1.8
Spermicides	1.7
Sponge	1

pills taken at specific intervals. This technique can be used if a woman has had unprotected intercourse because her method failed or she was sexually assaulted or for any number of reasons. The morning-after pill must be administered within hours of intercourse to be effective.

Oral Contraceptives

Birth control pills, or oral contraceptives, are very effective when used properly. There are two types of birth control pills: combination pills, containing the hormones estrogen and progestin, and mini-pills containing only progestin. Progestin is a synthetic version of the natural female hormone progesterone. Women use the combination pills most often; those women who cannot take estrogen use the mini-pill.

To be effective, the pill must be taken regularly. Some pills are taken daily during a 28-day cycle, whereas others are taken for 21 days, with no pills taken for 7 days before the next pack is started. Missing one pill can result in pregnancy. Birth control pills are generally safe for women in good health who do not smoke. There is no reason to have rest periods from oral contraceptives after they are taken for a number of years.

Aside from preventing pregnancy, birth control pills have other benefits. Oral contraceptives protect against cancer of the ovary and the endometrium. The longer a woman takes the pill, the greater the protective effect. Women who take the pill have a lower risk of ovarian cysts, ovarian and endometrial cancer, uterine fibroids, noncancerous breast disease, and ectopic pregnancies. They also tend to have more regular periods with less monthly flow and fewer premenstrual symptoms. The estrogen in oral contraceptives also appears to increase bone density, reducing the risk of bone loss that occurs during menopause.

On the other hand, oral contraceptives have been linked to certain types of cardiovascular disease and cancer of the breast. These effects were observed when higher dose formulations were in use and other factors linked to disease, such as smoking, were not taken into consideration. In general, today's low-dose pills do not seem to pose the same risk. There is, however, an increased risk of thromboembolism (blood clots) in women who smoke and take the pill. Although one study has shown a link between breast cancer and oral contraceptives, others have not been able to confirm that finding.

Oral contraceptives can be used by most healthy women. Do not take birth control pills, however, if any of the following factors apply to you:

- Age over 35 and smoke
- History of vascular disease (including stroke and thromboembolism)
- Uncontrolled high blood pressure, diabetes with vascular disease, high cholesterol
- Active liver disease
- Cancer of the endometrium or breast

Women over age 35 who do not smoke can continue to take a low-dose pill with safety until menopause. Some women may develop bloating, spotting, severe mood swings, or breast tenderness. These problems, or a tendency toward them, require that the woman and her physician work together to find the right formula for her.

Implants

Implants involve a new technique of inserting small plastic tubes containing a progestin or levonorgestrel just under the skin of the arm (see Fig. 2.11). After an injection of local anesthetic to numb the area, the small tubes are imbedded under the skin in the upper arm during an office visit. The hormone is slowly released over a 5-year period. This method of contraception is very effective, but it can cause irregular bleeding and spotting. Other side effects include weight gain, headache, acne, depression,

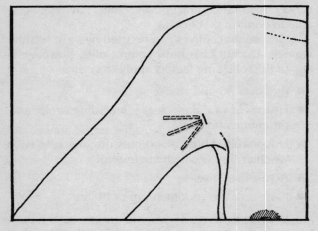

Figure 2.11   Implants
One of the newer methods of birth control is hormonal implants. These small, matchstick-sized tubes are inserted just beneath the surface of the skin, usually on the inner part of a woman's upper arm. The implants contain progestin, a synthetic form of the hormone progesterone, which is slowly released into the bloodstream to prevent pregnancy. Insertion can be done during an office visit, and the implants are effective for up to 5 years.

abnormal hair growth, anxiety, and ovarian cysts. The implants need to be surgically removed, and there have been reports that this sometimes can be difficult.

Injections
The injection technique involves injecting a long-acting type of progesterone into the body every 3 months; the failure rate is low. The side effects with this technique include abdominal discomfort, nervousness, dizziness, decreased sex drive, depression, and acne. Some women have weight gain. This method can disrupt menstrual cycles and cause episodes of bleeding and spotting.

Barrier Methods
Some, but not all, barrier methods provide protection against STDs. They can be used in combination to offer extra protection against pregnancy and STDs.

Diaphragm
The diaphragm is a reusable round rubber disk with a flexible rim that fits inside the vagina to cover the cervix (see Fig. 2.12). It should be coated with a spermicide before it is inserted into the vagina. The success of the diaphragm depends partly on spermicidal cream or jelly and partly on its function as a barrier to block entry of the sperm into the cervix. It must be fitted to the shape of the woman's vagina by a doctor or nurse.

The diaphragm should be inserted 1 hour before intercourse and should be left in place at least 6 hours after having sex. If intercourse is repeated, additional spermicide should be inserted into the vagina. When irritation occurs, it may be due to

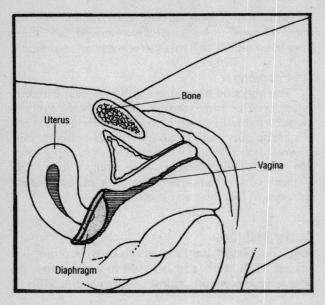

Figure 2.12 Diaphragm
One of the barrier methods of contraception is the diaphragm, a
rubber, dome-shaped device that is used with spermicide. It is
inserted into the vagina to hold the spermicide in place against the
cervix. The flexible rim of the diaphragm helps to hold it in place
behind the pubic bone.

either the rubber or the spermicide. Changing brands
of spermicide may solve this problem.

Cervical Cap

The cervical cap is similar to the diaphragm,
although it is smaller. Fitting snugly over the cervix, it
is held in place by suction (see Fig. 2.13). The cervical cap comes in 4 sizes to fit a woman's cervix. The
cervical cap can be difficult to insert, and it doesn't

fit all women. It can be left in a longer time than a diaphragm and can be used to contain menstrual fluid.

Condom

Condoms, for use by both men and women, are all available without prescription. They offer good protection against STDs, including the HIV infection that causes AIDS, as well as pregnancy when used properly. Condoms protect against both viral and bacterial infections, and their use lowers the risk of cancer of the cervix. With new sexual partners of

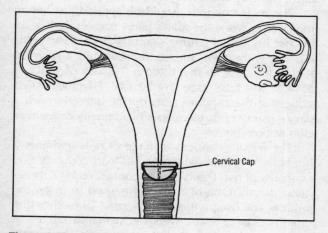

Figure 2.13   Cervical Cap
Similar to the diaphragm, the cervical cap is a small, cup-shaped, rubber device. Also used with spermicide, it is inserted into the vagina and pushed onto the cervix, where it is held in place by suction. The cap is somewhat more difficult to learn to place correctly than the diaphragm, but many women like it because it can be left in place longer and, for some, may be more comfortable.

unknown risk for STD, use condoms regardless of other contraceptive methods you may be using. Condoms are disposable; use them one time only and then discard.

The male condom is a sheath that fits over the erect penis and collects the sperm when a man ejaculates. Most condoms are made of latex rubber, although they can be made of animal intestines. Only latex rubber condoms protect against disease, however. Some condoms contain a spermicide (e.g., nonoynol) that immobilizes and kills the sperm, providing additional contraception. You can get extra protection by using a foam that contains spermicide along with the condom.

The male condom should be applied just before intercourse, when the man's penis is erect, before he touches his sexual partner's genitals. When the penis is being withdrawn, the condom should always be held at the base so that there is less risk of spillage, leakage, or tears (see Fig. 2.14). Effectiveness is reduced if the condom tears during intercourse. If a leak or tear occurs, use a spermicidal jelly or foam as soon as possible.

The female condom is made of polyurethane, a thin but strong material that resists tearing during use. It consists of two flexible rings connected by a loose-fitting sheath. One of the rings is used to insert the condom and hold it inside the vagina. The other ring remains outside and covers the woman's labia and the base of the penis during intercourse. The female condom is prelubricated and lines the vagina after insertion (see Fig. 2.15). It is designed for one-time use only. One advantage of the female condom is that it can be inserted several hours before sex. Its fairly high failure rate is often due to incorrect use. Used properly, the female condom is nearly as effective as other techniques.

Sponge

The sponge is available without a prescription; it is made of polyurethane and contains a spermicide. Before intercourse, the sponge is inserted into the vagina to cover the cervix, forming both a physical shield and chemical barrier to sperm. It should be left in place for at least 6 hours after intercourse. The

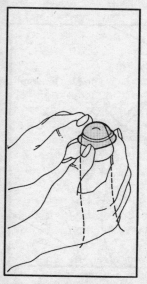
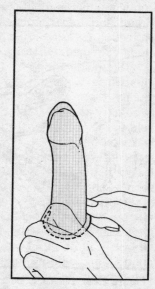

Figure 2.14 Male Condom
The male condom is one of the most widely used forms of contraception. It also offers protection against sexually transmitted diseases, including HIV, the virus that causes AIDS. The rolled-up condom is placed over the man's erect penis (A) and then unrolled downward (B). A small space is left at the tip of the condom to catch the man's semen during ejaculation.

sponge may be left in place up to 24 hours, and it is effective if intercourse is repeated during that time. As with diaphragms or condoms that contain spermicide, a small percentage of users may experience irritation or allergic reactions.

Intrauterine Devices

There are currently two types of intrauterine devices (IUD) available. One is a plastic device shaped like the letter *T* that is wound with copper, and the other

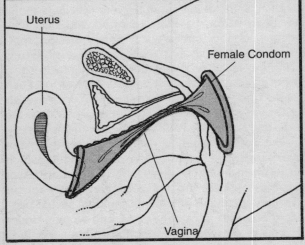

Figure 2.15 Female Condom
The newest form of barrier contraception, the female condom, also offers women protection against sexually transmitted diseases. It consists of a long rubber sheath with a closed ring at one end and a slightly larger, open ring at the other. The closed end is inserted into the vagina and fits over the cervix, like the diaphragm. The open end hangs outside the vagina, so that the interior of the vagina and the cervix are covered.

is a device that releases the hormone progesterone. When placed inside the uterus, the IUD causes an inflammatory reaction in the uterine lining that prevents pregnancy.

The IUD device must be put in place by a trained physician or nurse. It is inserted through the cervix into the uterus. Threads hang through the cervix and must be checked monthly after each period to be sure the IUD is still in place (see Fig. 2.16). The IUD containing progesterone should be replaced every year, while the copper-containing IUD can be used for 8 years.

Some women have uncomfortable short-term side effects, including cramping and dizziness at the time of insertion; bleeding, cramps, and backache that may continue for a few days after insertion; spotting between periods; and longer and heavier periods during the first few cycles after insertion. Use of a copper IUD increases the amount of blood lost each month, while use of the hormone IUD decreases it. The device can migrate into the muscular wall of the uterus and sometimes tear it, although this is rare.

The copper-releasing IUD increases the risk of developing pelvic inflammatory disease (PID), which can result in infertility, especially in those at risk of PID. These people are not good candidates for an IUD; they include women with multiple sexual partners, those with a history of PID, and women under 25 years of age who have not had children. An IUD is a good choice for women who have completed their families and are in monogamous sexual relationships.

Periodic Abstinence

Also known as natural family planning or the rhythm method, periodic abstinence relies on close observation of a woman's cycle to detect when ovulation occurs. Women using this method note the temperature increase that occurs just before ovulation and the change in cervical mucus from dry to wet and slippery that occurs around the same time. It takes into account the fact that sperm live an average of 5 days in the uterus and that the life span of the egg after ovulation is 1 to 3 days. In general, a couple should not have sexual intercourse 7 days before and 3 days after ovulation. Couples who use this method should obtain detailed instructions about it and follow the plan carefully. If used perfectly, this method can be

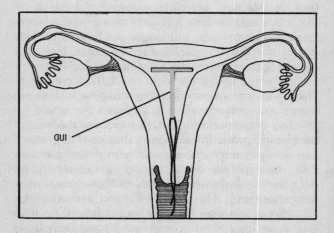

Figure 2.16   IUD
The intrauterine device (IUD) is a small, plastic device that is inserted into the uterus and left in place to prevent pregnancy. The two forms of IUD currently available are a T-shaped device wound with fine copper wire (shown here) and one containing the hormone progesterone.

very effective. It is less effective than other forms of birth control, however, because of the difficulty in predicting exactly when ovulation will occur.

Sterilization

Men and women who no longer wish to have children may choose to undergo sterilization. The technique for women is known as tubal ligation (see Fig. 2.17), and the one for men is called vasectomy. The procedure for male sterilization is less risky and less expensive than female sterilization (see "Conditions and Disorders in Men," page 111). Sterilization should be considered a permanent form of birth control, although in some cases it can be reversed.

Sterilization in women is usually done by laparoscopy. Laparoscopic surgery has been nicknamed Band-Aid surgery because of the small size of the incision near or through the navel.

For the procedure, gas is introduced into the abdominal cavity; the gas pushes the intestine away from the uterus and fallopian tubes. A lighted tube called a laparoscope is inserted through the same incision to allow the surgeon to view the internal area. Operating instruments can be inserted either through the laparoscope or through a second small incision at the pubic hair line. The fallopian tubes are then sealed with electric current that also stops bleeding. In some cases, a ring or clip can be inserted over the tubes through the laparoscope to seal them. Other reversible means of sealing the tubes are being explored.

The procedure is very effective in preventing pregnancy. Complications are rare but include injuries to the bowel or blood vessels and infection.

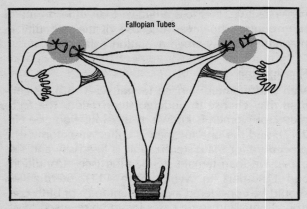

Figure 2.17 Tubal Ligation
Sterilization is a permanent form of birth control. In women, it is done by a procedure called tubal ligation, in which both fallopian tubes are cut and sealed by tying, banding, or clipping the cut ends. The egg released each month by one of the ovaries thus cannot be reached by the man's sperm.

Abortion

The medical term for termination of a pregnancy by any cause is *abortion*. The term *spontaneous abortion* describes a natural end of the pregnancy, also called a miscarriage, before the fetus is able to live outside the uterus (about the first 6 months of pregnancy). If a spontaneous abortion is incomplete—if some tissue is retained in the uterus—a medical procedure may be required to be sure the uterus has been emptied and there is no risk of infection. An *elective abortion* refers to the surgical or medical termination of a pregnancy. When a woman is ill and cannot withstand the strain of the pregnancy, termination may be called therapeutic abortion.

With any form of abortion, the initial step is confirming the pregnancy. Most commercially available pregnancy tests inform you of your pregnancy status at the time of the first missed menstrual period. Although this usually occurs about 2 weeks after conception, some women have a lighter period and are unaware they are pregnant until they miss the next period, approximately 6 weeks after the date of conception.

Elective abortions can be performed in a physician's office as early as 1 to 2 weeks after a missed menstrual period. Using the menstrual extraction technique, the contents of the uterus are removed with a syringe. After 7 weeks of pregnancy, doctors use a procedure called vacuum curettage, the most common method of abortion in the United States. Beyond 13 weeks of pregnancy, more involved procedures are required.

Before the procedure, a woman has her blood type checked and a pregnancy test repeated. She is counseled by health care workers about the procedure and given a chance to ask questions. Consent forms must be signed by the patient and may be required from others, depending on state law. In most cases, the patient is also examined to confirm the length of the pregnancy so the physician can determine the best way to perform the procedure.

Vacuum curettage is performed with a local anesthetic, injected into and around the cervix. The cervix is then dilated, or opened, using a series of gradually larger metal rods or a synthetic material that swells. The contents of the uterus are then removed with a suction device. As the uterus contracts to its previous size, some cramping may result. The amount of blood lost is usually small. In most clinics, only about 1 percent of women have complications such as infection, perforation of the uterus, or bleeding.

Abortions in later stages have a higher risk of complications and should be performed in a hospital or a specialized clinic. They can be done with suction or by administering agents that bring on labor. In some extreme cases, surgery may be required.

A drug called mifepristone can induce abortion; it is also known as the French pill, or RU–486 and is not currently available in this country. Efforts are ongoing to have this drug available so it can be offered as a safer, nonsurgical approach to abortion.

In the days when abortions were outlawed, women sought abortions from unlicensed providers who frequently did not use sterile techniques and who did not monitor women for complications. As a result, women developed advanced infections that spread from the uterus to the bloodstream and the abdominal cavity. Such infections could result in permanent sterility or death. Today, abortions are extremely safe when performed in a proper medical setting by a licensed practitioner. An abortion has no effect on a woman's ability to have children in the future.

Cancer Detection

When cancer develops in a woman's reproductive organs, it is rarely accompanied by symptoms. (See Fig. 2.18) In some cases, cancer can be prevented by detecting precancerous changes in the cells. In others, noncancerous conditions can cause symptoms that must be explored to rule out cancer. Although the initial evaluation can be done by a gynecologist, a gynecologic oncologist, who specializes in cancer of the reproductive organs, should provide care once cancer is diagnosed. The earlier cancer is detected and treated, the better the chance for cure.

Cervix

The Pap test can detect changes in the cells of the cervix that are not cancer but may warn that cancer could develop (see Fig. 2.10). Some of these changes return to normal on their own, whereas for others,

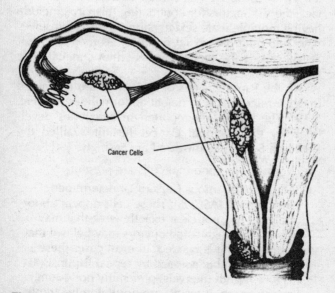

Cancer Cells

Figure 2.18 Cancer
Possible sites of cancer in women include the ovary, uterus, and cervix.

treatment can keep cancer from developing. The Pap test can allow almost all cases of cervical cancer to be prevented, which is why it is so important that you have one regularly.

There are virtually no symptoms during the earliest stage of cervical cancer. The most common early warning signs of cervical cancer are spotting or irregular bleeding or bleeding after intercourse. These signs should prompt an immediate visit to a gynecologist.

Risk factors for cervical cancer include early age at first intercourse, having multiple sexual partners, smoking, and infection with human papillomavirus (HPV). Because HPV is spread through sexual contact, the risk factors for contracting this virus include having multiple male sexual partners who themselves have had multiple sexual partners. Women are most at risk during the teenage years when cervical cells are maturing.

In the Pap test, cells of the cervix are examined under a microscope to detect abnormalities (see Fig. 2.19). The results are reported in categories developed by the National Cancer Institute, called the Bethesda System, and treated accordingly:

- Normal: No abnormal cells are present.

- Atypical Squamous Cells of Undetermined Significance (ASCUS): These cells appear abnormal, but it is not clear exactly what that may mean. Although some doctors may believe that further testing is needed, in most cases these changes can be assessed by repeat Pap tests at 3- to 6-month intervals, preferably not during menstruation. If results are normal in two consecutive tests, annual Pap tests can be resumed and no further treatment is needed. About 70

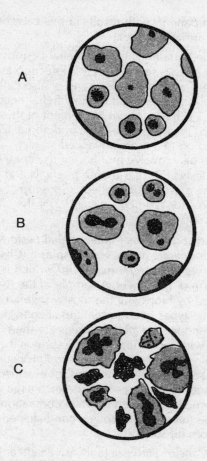

Figure 2.19   Pap Test
In the Pap test, cells collected from the cervix are examined under a microscope to detect abnormalities. Shown here are normal cervical cells (A), cells showing cervical dysplasia (B), and typical cancer cells (C).

percent of patients with results in this category need no further treatment.

- Low-Grade Squamous Intraepithelial Lesions: Includes changes seen with HPV infection as well as early precancerous changes, also called mild dysplasia or cervical intraepithelial neoplasia grade 1 (CIN 1). About 60 percent of these changes go away on their own, and about 15 percent go on to a more advanced stage. Follow-up may involve monitoring the condition with Pap tests at 3- to 6-month intervals and performing a procedure called colposcopy (see "Procedures for Women," page 102) if the condition persists.

- High-Grade Squamous Intraepithelial Lesions: Includes moderate and severe dysplasia (CIN 2 and 3) as well as carcinoma in situ, which is a severe form of precancer. A sample of the tissue is obtained by biopsying the most severe area to confirm the types of abnormalities seen through the colposcope. The affected areas are then removed with local surgery using various techniques: loop electrosurgical excision procedure (LEEP), laser, freezing techniques, or electrosurgery (see "Procedures for Women," page 102). A procedure called cervical conization may be performed to remove a cone-shaped wedge from the cervix.

- Invasive Cancer: Early stage invasive cancer can be treated with either hysterectomy (removal of the uterus) or radiation therapy. In later stages, especially when the lymph nodes are involved, a combination of surgery, radiation, and possibly chemotherapy may be used.

There is a 90 percent likelihood that the treatment for early precancerous changes will completely remove any abnormal tissue. About 10 percent of women have an abnormal Pap smear during that first year after treatment. Treatment of this persistent area has a cure rate of about 90 percent. Thus, there is about a 99 percent cure rate with two treatments. Women who have been treated should continue to have yearly Pap tests, however, even after menopause or hysterectomy.

Uterus

Cancer of the lining of the uterus, the endometrium, is the most common gynecologic cancer. About 31,000 cases occur annually. The survival rate for this cancer is high if the cancer is diagnosed in a very early stage.

The most frequent symptom of endometrial cancer is spotting or irregular bleeding, which should alert a woman to seek treatment. Women in the menopausal years should consult their physicians immediately if they develop spotting after their regular periods have stopped for 1 year or more.

The greatest risk factor for endometrial cancer appears to be excess amounts of the hormone estrogen. Estrogen stimulates the uterine lining to grow, causing a condition called endometrial hyperplasia, a form of precancer. The excess estrogen can come from a variety of sources:

- Hormone replacement therapy taken during and after menopause includes estrogen and progesterone. If estrogen is taken alone, a woman's risk of developing endometrial cancer is increased. By taking both estrogen and progesterone pills, however, a woman's risk of cancer is even lower than those who take no therapy.

■ Fat cells are the most abundant source of excess estrogen production. Some fat cells normally convert inactive adrenal hormones into very active estrogenlike hormones. These hormones overstimulate the uterine lining to grow, possibly out of control, into cancer. Women who are slightly overweight have a threefold risk of developing endometrial cancer and those who are nearly twice their recommended weight have a tenfold risk of developing endometrial cancer.

The diagnosis is confirmed by performing a uterine biopsy to obtain a sample of the lining to study. This procedure can be performed in a physician's office, without any anesthesia. The "D&C," or dilation and curettage, is rarely needed now that suction biopsies can be done in the office.

Treatment usually consists of a hysterectomy. The

STAGING OF ENDOMETRIAL CANCER

Stage I	Cancer confined to the body of the uterus.
Stage II	Cancer extended from the body of the uterus to the cervix.
Stage III	Cancer spread out to lymph nodes or onto the ovaries.
Stage IV	Distant spread to the lung or into the bladder or rectum.

ovaries are usually removed (oophorectomy), along with the lymph nodes. A careful search is made for any sign of further spread (see "Staging of Endometrial Cancer"). A general gynecologist can perform the surgery in early stage cancer but a gynecologic oncologist should always be available if advanced disease is found during the surgery. If advanced disease is diagnosed preoperatively, the gynecologic oncologist should perform the surgery. After surgery and complete pathological evaluation of the uterus, the ovaries, and the lymph nodes, further treatment may be recommended in the form of either radiation or chemotherapy.

Ovarian Cancer

Ovarian cancer is the most malignant of all of the gynecologic cancers. Approximately 24,000 women develop ovarian cancer each year, and unfortunately many are not diagnosed until the cancer is in advanced stages. The risk factors for ovarian cancer include advanced age, not having children or having them late in life, and a family history of ovarian cancer or other cancers such as breast or colon cancers.

Ovarian cancer gives only vague early warning signs, such as a change in bowel pattern, a feeling of bloating, or simply pelvic discomfort. These symptoms may be due to pressure from a pelvic mass or tumor implants on the bowel wall.

When ovarian cancer grows, some women think they are only getting fat and don't investigate the cause of the swelling. The cancer can cause fluid to accumulate within the abdominal cavity, causing the abdomen to swell. This fluid contains cancer cells and can spread even into the lung cavity, where more fluid can accumulate.

Since there are so few warning signs in the early stages, this cancer is usually diagnosed later, when tumor nodules from the ovaries extend to the surface of the liver, the bowel, the stomach, or inside the abdominal wall. Cancer is often suspected by pelvic exam and confirmed by ultrasound. A blood test also can be performed to measure a substance called CA–125 that circulates in the blood. CA–125 is used as a tumor marker because levels are increased when tumors are present. Because levels are increased by the presence of many other benign disorders, this test is not used to screen healthy women.

Therapy usually begins with surgery to remove all the tumor, followed by chemotherapy. The chemotherapy is fairly effective at removing any tumor cells left after surgery. While a complete cure of this cancer occurs in only about 20–30 percent of women, chemotherapy usually prolongs life very significantly.

Ovarian Cysts

Often a cyst may develop on an ovary. This fluid-filled growth is not cancerous in most cases. Some may be the earliest sign that a cancer has formed, however, so all ovarian cysts should be taken seriously and evaluated. Ovarian cysts may have no symptoms; large cysts can cause a feeling of pelvic pressure or fullness. Diagnosis is usually by vaginal ultrasound: A small probe is passed into the vagina that reveals details of the ovaries and uterus. The CA–125 blood test can also be performed to assess the likelihood of ovarian cancer. Treatment of ovarian cysts ranges from careful monitoring of simple small cysts to surgical removal of any ovarian cysts that may suggest a malignancy. Oral contraceptives do not make an ovarian cyst disappear any faster. If you have an ovarian cyst that is under observation, your doctor should check it again within 3 months to make sure it has not changed or grown larger. Always get a second opinion before having surgery for an ovarian cyst.

Vagina

Cancer of the vagina that does not involve the vulva or the cervix is rare. One form is caused by exposure to a drug called diethylstilbestrol, or DES, in women whose mothers took the drug while they were pregnant. In the early 1950s DES was prescribed to women who were at risk of losing their pregnancies. Now, their daughters are at risk for some cancers of the vagina. A registry has been created to keep track of these women so they can receive careful monitoring. The cancer usually develops around age 19; treatment is by hysterectomy, and it has a 90 percent cure rate if identified in the earliest stage of growth.

Vulva

Vulvar cancer is a rare gynecologic malignancy. It almost always strikes women who are in the menopausal years and appears to be linked to infection with HPV. The cancer appears as a small sore or small lump on one of the outer lips of the vulva. Sometimes it can itch, but it usually does not cause any pain. Many women delay seeing their gynecologists, hoping the sore will disappear; however, this delay allows for continued tumor growth. If you have a small sore, lump, or ulcer on any area of the vulva that is new and does not go away within a week, see your physician.

The diagnosis is based on the results of a biopsy, in which the area is numbed and a small amount of tissue is removed to be studied. If the cancer is found in early stages, surgery is performed. Usually, the area of cancer must be removed with a rim of normal tissue of approximately 1 inch in diameter all the way around the cancer. This is called a radical partial vulvectomy. In most stages of disease, lymph nodes in the groin should also be removed. If cancer has spread to the lymph nodes, radiation therapy is usually required.

Ectopic Pregnancy

Normally, once the egg is fertilized in the fallopian tubes, it travels to the uterus and becomes implanted there. When, for any reason, the fertilized egg implants anywhere else along the route, the pregnancy is said to be ectopic, or in the wrong place (see Fig. 2.20).

Ectopic pregnancy occurs when the opening of the fallopian tube is twisted or narrowed, due to scar tissue formed by infection or surgery. The passage of the fertilized egg to the uterus is blocked, and the egg begins to develop within the fallopian tube lining, on the surface of the ovary, or within the abdominal or pelvic cavity. The egg can only develop for a few weeks before its growth is hindered by the size of the fallopian tube.

In an ectopic pregnancy, symptoms of early pregnancy, an abnormally light period, and pelvic pain can occur. Many women have no symptoms until the pregnancy causes a rupture of the fallopian tube or there is bleeding from a nearby blood vessel. This

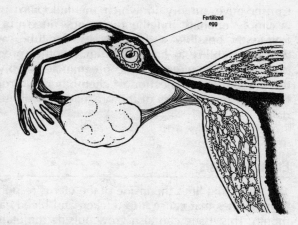

Figure 2.20   Ectopic Pregnancy
In an ectopic pregnancy, the fertilized ovum becomes attached in a place other than inside the uterus. Most ectopic pregnancies occur in a fallopian tube.

causes severe abdominal pain, shock, and collapse—a medical emergency of the first order.

If you have a history of tubal infections or previous ectopic pregnancy and suspect you are pregnant, you should be carefully monitored by your physician to be sure that the pregnancy is within the uterus. Ectopic pregnancy is diagnosed by doing tests to measure hormone levels that indicate pregnancy. Once pregnancy has been confirmed, ultrasound can determine its location and size.

If the fallopian tube has ruptured, the condition is an emergency that requires surgery to remove the pregnancy and control bleeding. In some cases, the tube can then be rejoined. Many surgeons are now performing this procedure through the laparoscope.

Conservative surgery in which the fallopian tube is simply opened and the pregnancy lifted out is frequently possible and conserves the tube, and thus your ability to have children. Another procedure for small, early ectopic pregnancies involves the intramuscular injection of chemotherapy drugs; the usual result is loss of the pregnancy in about 7 days.

Endometriosis

The tissue that lines the inside of the uterus responds to hormones that cause it to thicken and bleed each month. This tissue can also grow outside the uterus, on the pelvic organs. When this occurs, these areas can become inflamed and sometimes painful, and scar tissue develops.

Some women with endometriosis, even severe endometriosis, have no symptoms. Others can have intense pain, especially when the endometrial tissue is shed into the pelvic area during the menstrual period. The pain can be felt throughout the entire area or may be confined to the uterus. Pain usually appears only during the menstrual period, but can start just before and gradually increase until bleeding starts, usually easing after up to 72 hours. In addition to pelvic pain, endometriosis is a common cause of infertility because it causes the fallopian tubes to malfunction.

Researchers have not been able to pinpoint causes of endometriosis. One theory is that endometrial tissue travels through the fallopian tubes and becomes implanted on surrounding structures (see Fig. 2.21). Delay of pregnancy to beyond age 30 is associated

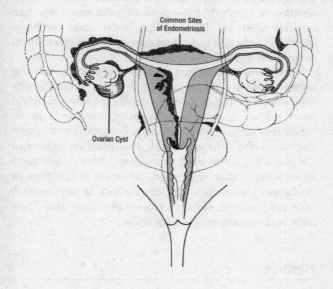

Figure 2.21   Endometriosis
Endometriosis is a condition in which tissue similar to that lining
the uterus is present outside the uterus. It may be attached to the
outside of the uterus, ovaries, or tubes, or it may be present in
other areas of the abdomen.

with a higher risk of endometriosis. Women who have
never had a pregnancy are at highest risk.

Laparoscopy is used for both definitive diagnosis
and treatment of endometriosis. The treatment of
endometriosis depends largely on the patient's needs
and desires. If relief of pain is of most importance and
childbearing has been completed, a hysterectomy

with removal of the ovaries, followed by hormone replacement therapy, is often recommended. When fertility is desired, the spots of endometriosis can be removed by laparoscopy with laser therapy. Unfortunately, the condition recurs in about one third of women treated.

Synthetic hormones can be used to shrink the endometriosis implants, but the effect is temporary. The implants usually return to their premedication level within a few months after treatment ends. Treatment can be given for only 6 months because it decreases the estrogen level. This brief remission of the disease can be time enough to allow conception soon after, if that is desired. Because prevention of ovulation can reduce the discomfort, many women take oral contraceptives. However, some still have pain and require surgery for relief.

Fibroids

Benign fibrous growths of the uterine wall are called fibroids. Some fibroids bulge outward from the wall; others extend from the uterine surface on a stalk. A fibroid can also extend into the uterine lining, compressing the endometrium or forming a growth on a stem within the endometrial cavity. About 20 percent of women of reproductive age have fibroids, and for most of them the fibroids pose no problem.

Fibroids enlarge the uterus and can cause pressure and discomfort in the pelvis, however. Internal uterine fibroids can also compress the endometrial lining and cause excessive bleeding during and occasionally between menstrual periods. Younger women rarely have fibroids, but when they do, the fibroids can press against the lining of the uterus causing infertility. The most serious complication is pressure and blockage of the ureters, the tubes draining the kidneys. On rare occasions, a fibroid can develop into a malignant tumor. Fibroids have been the most common reason for hysterectomy in the past, as well as currently. The only reason for removing the fibroids or for doing a hysterectomy for fibroids is if they cause symptoms like bladder or pelvic pressure, excessive bleeding, infertility, or pain.

Ultrasound is used to determine the size and location of fibroids. Two types of surgery, if needed, are used to remove the growths:

- Hysterectomy to remove the uterus and with it, the fibroids
- Myomectomy to remove the fibroids only, leaving the uterus intact

The selection of the type of surgery used rests with the woman and her surgeon. For a woman who wants to maintain her fertility, a myomectomy is the treatment of choice. It might also be preferred by the woman who wishes to have her uterus and ovaries left intact.

Myomectomy usually involves more blood loss than a hysterectomy, because the fibroid can have a rich blood supply. During a hysterectomy, the location of each blood vessel that feeds the uterus is well known and can be clamped off so that little bleeding occurs. During myomectomy, the blood supply to the fibroid is less clearly defined and blood loss can be heavy. Many gynecologists recommend that women who do not want to retain fertility simply have the top half or the entire uterus removed in what is called a partial hysterectomy.

Sometimes this procedure can be made easier by shrinking the fibroid prior to surgery. This is done by prescribing hormones that mimic menopause and decrease the amount of estrogens, resulting in shrinkage of the fibroid by as much as 50 percent.

Women can usually become pregnant after removal of a fibroid and carry the pregnancy to full term, although they may occasionally require a delivery.

Menopause

At menopause, a woman stops menstruating and her ovaries no longer produce estrogen. The average age at the last menstrual period is 51. This natural process begins several years before, as a woman's ovaries produce less and less estrogen. The lack of estrogen can produce a number of effects:

- Hot flashes or flushes can occur. These are sudden feelings of heat that spread over the body, often accompanied by a flushed face and sweating. They appear at any time without warning and are most troublesome at night when they can interfere with sleep.

- Vaginal tissues may become dryer, thinner, and less flexible. This can result in painful intercourse, urinary tract problems, or sagging of pelvic organs because the tissues that support them lose their elasticity.

- Osteoporosis, or bone loss, can cause bones to become thin and brittle. Supplemental estrogen can help guard against it, as can a diet high in calcium, regular exercise, and stopping smoking.

- Cardiovascular disease becomes more of a risk for women after menopause because estrogen no longer gives them natural protection from heart attack and stroke.

- Emotional changes such as mood swings, irritability, and depression can accompany menopause, but these symptoms are more likely related to insomnia caused by hot flashes at night than to the lack of estrogen.

Not all women have all of these symptoms and they are not always long lasting. You can continue to have a full and healthy life for many years beyond menopause. Some of the symptoms of menopause can be eased through diet and exercise. Others can be relieved by replacing the estrogen no longer produced by the ovaries. Hormone replacement therapy can relieve the symptoms of menopause, in addition to lowering the risk of heart disease and osteoporosis.

Estrogen is given along with the hormone progestin (a synthetic version of the natural hormone progesterone) to protect against endometrial cancer, a risk when estrogen is taken alone. Estrogen by itself causes the lining of the uterus to overgrow and increases the risk of cancer of the endometrium. Progestin is taken with estrogen to oppose it and keep the lining of the endometrium in check. In fact, taking progestin with estrogen actually lowers the risk of cancer to less than that of a woman not taking hormone therapy.

Estrogen is processed through the liver and affects the levels of cholesterol. Estrogen increases high-density cholesterol (the good cholesterol) and lowers low-density cholesterol (the bad cholesterol), thus reducing the risk of heart disease. Without estrogen, a woman's risk of heart disease approaches that of a man by age 65.

Women are at higher risk of osteoporosis because they have less bone mass than men to begin with and because they tend to have less calcium stored in their bones. Thus, when they lose the protective effect of estrogen, the natural process of bone loss speeds up so they are losing bone faster than it is being replaced.

Osteoporosis and cardiovascular disease do not have symptoms in their early stages as they are conditions that develop over time. Hormone replacement therapy to prevent symptoms of menopause also helps prevent these conditions. To provide long-term protection, the therapy must be taken long term.

Hormone replacement therapy is not for everyone. It is not recommended for women who have had breast cancer, endometrial cancer, or liver cancer. The link between breast cancer and hormone replacement therapy is still not clear. There may be a slight increase in a woman's chance of developing breast cancer if she has been taking hormones for more than 15 years.

Hormone replacement therapy can have other side effects. The progestin causes monthly bleeding or spotting that can be unexpected and bothersome. Other side effects include breast tenderness, fluid retention, swelling, mood changes, and pelvic cramping. Because of the side effects, some women choose to take estrogen alone. These women should be monitored carefully for abnormal bleeding. Their doctors may suggest that an endometrial biopsy be performed so a small amount of tissue can be examined.

Women who prefer not to take hormone replacement therapy can obtain relief of symptoms and help prevent bone loss and heart disease in other ways. To facilitate decisions about hormones, women should have a fasting cholesterol test and a bone density test. Estrogen cream, used in the vagina, can treat vaginal dryness. A balanced diet rich in calcium and low in fat, regular exercise, and avoiding alcohol and tobacco can help reduce the rate of bone loss and protect against heart disease. Regardless of age or whether they are taking hormone replacement therapy, women should continue to have regular pelvic exams, mammograms, and Pap tests after they reach menopause.

Menstrual Problems

Most women experience some discomfort with their menstrual periods. Certain conditions, such as endometriosis or fibroids, can increase pain during menstrual periods. Any severe pain, unusual spotting or bleeding, or missed menstrual periods could be a sign of a problem that requires medical attention.

Amenorrhea

Amenorrhea is the absence of menstruation. This absence is normal before puberty, after menopause, and during pregnancy. Primary amenorrhea occurs when a woman reaches the age of 18 and has never had a period. It is usually caused by a problem in the endocrine system that regulates hormones. Secondary amenorrhea is present when a woman has had regular periods that stop for longer than 12 months. Amenorrhea may be triggered by a wide range of events:

Primary amenorrhea

- Ovarian failure
- Problems in the nervous system or the pituitary gland in the endocrine system that affect maturation at puberty
- Birth defects in which the reproductive structures do not develop properly

Secondary amenorrhea

- Problems that affect estrogen levels, such as stress, weight loss, exercise, or illness
- Problems affecting the pituitary, thyroid, or adrenal gland
- Ovarian tumors or surgical removal of the ovaries

To diagnose and treat amenorrhea it may be necessary to consult a reproductive endocrinologist. Treatment is based on the problem diagnosed. Blood tests are usually performed, and many patients are asked to keep a record of their early morning temperatures to detect the rise in temperature that occurs with ovulation.

Cramps

The sensation of spasmodic cramping or a feeling of chronic achy fullness can occur with a normal menstrual cycle and a normal anatomy. The pain is due to uterine contractions, caused by substances called prostaglandins.

Prostaglandins circulate within the blood. They can cause diarrhea by speeding up the contractions of the intestinal tract and lower blood pressure by relaxing the muscles of blood vessels. Thus many women frequently notice that severe menstrual pain is associated with mild diarrhea and occasionally an overall sensation of faintness in which they become pale, sweaty, and sometimes nauseated. Some women actually have fainting spells because of the low blood pressure resulting from the action of prostaglandins.

To relieve cramps, your doctor may recommend drugs called prostaglandin inhibitors or nonsteroidal anti-inflammatory drugs (NSAIDs), which are available without a prescription. Taking medication immediately at the onset of any symptoms usually results in dramatic improvement or complete relief. Taking these drugs even before symptoms begin may help, too. Relief also may be obtained by applications of heat and mild exercise.

Excessive Bleeding

Some women experience a menopause characterized by irregular, unpredictable, often heavy bleeding. If you develop severe irregular bleeding as you approach menopause, or experience new bleeding a year after your final period, your doctor should do a biopsy to confirm that no precancerous changes have taken place. This biopsy does not need to be the traditional dilation and curettage (D&C) that is performed in a hospital under general anesthesia. Rather, the biopsy is a simple procedure that takes place in the doctor's office. A slender, soft plastic canula is inserted through the cervix and a small sample of uterine tissue is obtained. The cost of this biopsy is about 10 percent of the cost of a regular D&C and provides the same information. These tests are 99.5 percent reliable in diagnosing a precancerous condition or cancer, if present. If there is no sign of cancer, excessive bleeding can be treated with hormone therapy or surgery on the lining of the uterus.

Pelvic Inflammatory Disease

Infection with the STDs chlamydia and gonorrhea can lead to pelvic inflammatory disease (PID). In PID, infection spreads upward through the cervix, the uterus, and the fallopian tubes into the pelvic cavity. White blood cells battling the infection cause a puslike discharge to surround the ovaries. The body tries to wall off this infection by creating filmy adhesions (a fibrous wall) from organ to organ to limit the spread of the infection. The adhesions can distort the fallopian tubes and result in infertility.

Early symptoms of PID include pelvic pain associated with fever and weakness; there also may be a vaginal discharge. If the infection continues, an abscess can form within the pelvis. The typical PID attack strikes after a menstrual period and begins with pelvic pain. Motion, even walking, can be painful. If the abscess develops, it can send bacteria into the bloodstream, causing high fever, chills, joint infections, and even death.

Diagnosis usually is based on the symptoms and presence of the abscess. In some cases, a sample of the discharge from the abscess can be used to identify the organism causing the infection. Antibiotics can stop the infection before an abscess has formed, if treatment is started early. If the infection is severe, some patients may require intravenous antibiotics in a hospital setting. Surgery may be necessary to drain an abscess, but it is usually not necessary to remove the uterus, tubes, and ovaries.

Premenstrual Syndrome

The regular, recurring symptoms that occur just prior to menstruation are called premenstrual syndrome (PMS). PMS is not a disease but rather a collection of symptoms that disappear once the menstrual period has begun.

Nearly all menstruating women experience a set of symptoms that tells them their periods are coming. For some women, these symptoms can be quite severe, involving a combination of emotional and physical changes. Emotional changes may include anger, anxiety, confusion, mood swings, tension, crying, depression, and an inability to concentrate. Physical symptoms include bloating, swollen breasts, fatigue, constipation, headache, and clumsiness.

The diagnosis rests on confirming the cyclic nature of these symptoms and ruling out any underlying psychological or physical dysfunction. Many women are asked to chart their symptoms so they can be related to the menstrual cycle to detect a pattern. The symptoms usually occur about 7 days before a menstrual period and go away once it begins.

The cause of PMS is unknown, despite extensive research into abnormal types of hormones that are secreted at this time, unusual ratios of one hormone to another, and imbalance between sodium and body water retention. Many theories have been studied, but none has been shown to be the primary cause. As a result, the condition is difficult to treat.

Treatment is generally aimed at relieving symptoms. Keeping a calendar and being aware of when symptoms occur helps most women; simply knowing their distressing symptoms are related to the onset of their periods can have a calming effect. There are other things you can try to ease symptoms of PMS:

- Dietary changes provide relief for some women: Decreasing sodium, sugar, caffeine, and alcohol; increasing complex carbohydrates; and eating smaller, more frequent meals.

- Dietary supplementation of calcium, magnesium, and vitamins B_6 and E may reduce symptoms.

- Exercise has been shown to help in depression and, theoretically, may be of some benefit for PMS.

- Diuretics can relieve the feeling of bloating and swelling caused by fluid retention.

- Pain can be relieved with nonsteroidal anti-inflammatory drugs (NSAIDs).

- Oral contraceptives are helpful in relieving symptoms in some women.

- Severe breast tenderness can be relieved by taking bromocriptine, a drug that stops the production of certain hormones, but this drug does not help other PMS symptoms.

Many medications have been tried with limited success. Some of them are expensive and most have side effects. It may be necessary to combine some remedies on a trial and error basis, along with modifications in diet and exercise.

Rape

Rape is sexual intercourse by force; it is epidemic in our country. This violent crime has both psychological as well as medical aspects that affect women's health.

A rape should be reported within 48 hours of its occurrence, as crucial evidence of it is more difficult to obtain after that time. Women should not wash, bathe, urinate, defecate, drink, or take any medication prior to reporting a rape. A practitioner experienced in this area should perform a thorough exam so there is evidence available if charges are brought against the accused rapist.

A physician first asks the woman to describe what happened and then examines her clothing for damage, taking particular note if there are any materials such as soil or stains such as body fluids sticking to the clothing. The physician next asks if any drugs or alcohol were taken by the woman or the rapist, because this may become an important issue during court procedures.

The physical exam consists of looking for evidence on the whole body, even though not every woman who has been raped has been physically injured. The physician measures and charts all injuries and may photograph them, looking carefully for bite marks, bruises, grip marks, and scratches. Samples are taken of the vaginal fluid to check for infection or sperm. Mouth swabs and saliva samples are obtained to look for bacteria and semen and possibly to perform DNA studies of the sample. Urine samples may be obtained to determine whether drugs were involved. Blood samples are obtained to test for HIV as well as hepatitis. If the HIV test is negative, another HIV test should be done in 6 months to determine whether the virus was contracted during the rape. A woman may be given treatment against possible STDs, and she should be offered emergency contraception if there is a chance pregnancy could result from the assault.

After the exam, comfort, support, and counseling are key to complete recovery. There are many groups available to counsel women who are recovering from previous molestation or rape.

Vaginitis

The internal environment of the vagina consists of a delicate balance of organisms that, along with normal vaginal secretions, keep it healthy and clean. When that balance is disrupted by an infection, a health problem, or some type of irritation, vaginitis can occur. Bacteria or yeast that grows normally in the vagina can overgrow and cause itching, redness, and pain in the vaginal area. Infections from other organisms, as well as allergic reactions, can also cause vaginitis.

Abnormal itching or any new discharge accompanied by an odor could be a sign of a vaginal infection. The characteristics of the discharge—its color, odor, and amount—can be a clue to the cause. Yeast is the most common cause of vaginitis, but bacteria and parasites can also cause it. The cause of vaginitis must be identified for treatment to be effective.

Bacterial Vaginosis

Among the more common vaginal infections, bacterial vaginosis is caused by the *Gardnerella, Bacteriodes,* and *Peptostreptococcus* bacteria. The primary symptom is a foul-smelling, profuse, watery vaginal discharge.

The diagnosis is confirmed by microscopic examination of the discharge. Treatment for this infection is the antibiotic metronidazole. Often, the infection recurs; longer treatment may be needed to prevent recurrences.

Yeast Infection

Some women are unusually susceptible to this most common of all vaginal infections. The cause may be a recent course of antibiotics that can decrease the normal vaginal bacteria and allow for an overgrowth of yeast. Other conditions, like diabetes and HIV infection, are also associated with recurrent yeast infections.

Your doctor will want to confirm that yeast is the cause by examining the vaginal discharge under a microscope. Discuss multiple recurrent yeast infections with your physician, because other problems such as diabetes should be ruled out.

Once you can recognize the symptoms of yeast vaginitis, you can treat yourself by purchasing any one of the over-the-counter antifungal creams or suppository preparations. Treatment is also available in pill form by prescription.

PROCEDURES FOR WOMEN

Cryotherapy

Cryotherapy involves freezing cells on the cervix to remove abnormal cells. Freezing kills cells but does not remove them from the vagina. The dead cells dissolve into the vaginal fluid and are washed away in the normal secretions. This can cause an increased vaginal discharge for about 2 weeks after the procedure.

Colposcopy

In colposcopy, the cervix, vagina, and vulva skin are examined systematically under microscopic magnification. When abnormal areas are detected, a sample is taken for further examination (a biopsy).

During the procedure, a speculum is inserted in the vagina to spread the vaginal walls, and a vinegar solution is sprayed into the cervix. The abnormal surface cells appear white, and normal cells remain pink. The entire area is examined, and a biopsy of any white area is performed.

Most women have a slight cramp for a minute or so during the biopsy. Otherwise, this procedure requires no anesthesia and is well tolerated. If a woman has severe cramps with her menstrual cycle, medication can be given before the exam to reduce discomfort.

Occasionally a scraping of tissue is obtained from the inner lining of the cervix beyond the limits of the area that can be seen. This scraping provides extra assurance that the entire abnormality has been identified. Once the biopsy results are available, therapy can be started.

Dilation and Curettage

Often referred to as a D&C, dilation and curettage removes the lining and contents of the uterus. Once the cervix is widened by dilators, the uterine lining is scraped out with a curette, a spoonlike instrument. A D&C is used to perform abortions, remove the lining of the uterus in cases of severe bleeding, or test for uterine cancer (see Fig. 2.22). A D&C is performed in a hospital or an ambulatory surgery center using general anesthetic. Rapid recovery with minimal spotting for 1 to 2 days can be expected. It has largely been replaced by the office biopsy.

Hysterectomy

A complete or total hysterectomy is removal of the entire uterus with the cervix (see Fig. 2.23A). A partial hysterectomy involves removing only a portion of the uterus (see Fig. 2.23B). A radical hysterectomy involves the removal of the uterus, cervix, lymph nodes, and other support structures around the cervix and uterus (see Fig. 2.23C). A hysterectomy can be performed through the vagina or through a cut in the abdomen, depending on the reasons for the surgery.

Reasons for performing a hysterectomy should be clearly understood prior to the procedure. Following are the most common reasons for a hysterectomy:

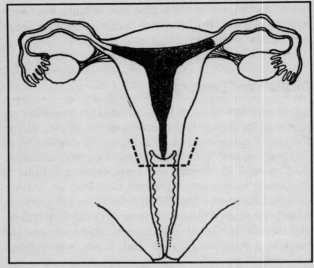

Figure 2.22. Dilation and Curettage
Dilation and curettage (D&C) is a procedure used to remove the endometrium (the lining of the uterus) and the contents of the uterus. A speculum is inserted into the vagina, the cervix is grasped with a small tonguelike instrument, and the inside of the uterus is gently scraped out with another instrument.

- Fibroids
- Endometriosis
- Cancer
- Endometrial hyperplasia
- Menstrual/menopausal symptoms
- Cervical dysplasia
- Pain

A vertical incision in the lower abdomen is used for abdominal hysterectomy or for cancer or a very large fibroid. For other conditions, a horizontal incision is placed just above the pubic bone, which can be hidden in the pubic hair (see Fig. 2.24). This location results in less postoperative pain.

A vaginal hysterectomy involves less discomfort than an abdominal hysterectomy, because no abdominal incision must be made. Vaginal hysterectomies are seldom performed on women who have had no children because the ligaments are tighter and the vaginal passage is small. It is indicated when there is a small uterus and the patient has had children, because the vagina and the connecting structures of the uterus are more pliable.

Vaginal hysterectomy is now available to more women because it can be done with a laparoscope. When the laparoscope is used, it is placed into the abdomen through a small incision in the abdominal wall. The laparoscope is a telescopelike probe that can identify the structures and treat problems outside the uterus, such as adhesions. The uterus can then be removed through the vagina with less postoperative pain and scarring.

Recovery time varies depending on the procedure. Usually, normal activities, including sex, can be resumed in about 4 to 6 weeks. Until then, activities such as driving, sports, and light physical work may be increased gradually. Adhesions, or scar tissue, can develop after any surgery. They can cause pain during bowel function, intercourse, or exercise. If adhesions are particularly troublesome, laparoscopic surgery can be used to relieve them, although they may return in the future.

After having had a hysterectomy, very few women notice a change in their sexual sensations that could be related to the functions of the uterus

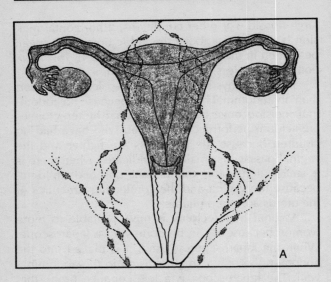

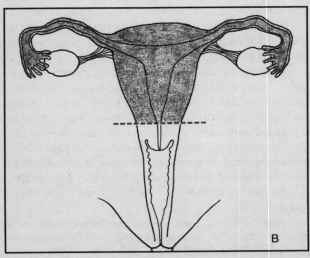

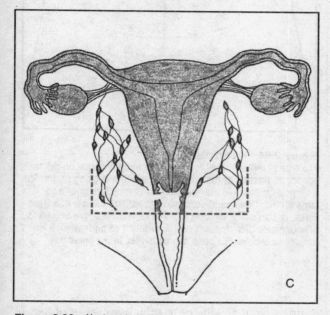

Figure 2.23 Hysterectomy

Hysterectomy, the surgical removal of the uterus, may be done in a number of ways, depending on the problem being treated. A total hysterectomy (A) involves the removal of the entire uterus, along with the ovaries and fallopian tubes. In a partial hysterectomy (B), the uterus and tubes are removed, but the ovaries and cervix are left in place. A radical hysterectomy (C) entails removal of the entire uterus, the tubes, and the ovaries, along with the lymph nodes and the support structures surrounding these organs.

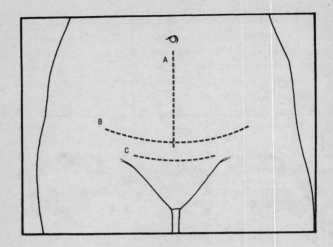

Figure 2.24 Hysterectomy Incisions
The type of incision used for a hysterectomy depends on the reason for and nature of the problem for which it is being performed. A vertical incision (A) may be used for uterine cancer or a very large fibroid. Other conditions may necessitate the use of a transverse, or horizontal, incision (B). The location and size of a transverse incision also depends on the problem being treated; a low transverse incision (C) often can be hidden in the pubic hair.

during sexual activity or to their own sense of loss of their uterus. For most women, hysterectomy has no effect on sexual satisfaction. Many women have a sense of freedom from symptoms of the condition corrected, as well as from the concern of monthly periods and potential pregnancy. If you have any doubts about having a hysterectomy, always get a second opinion.

Hysteroscopy

Hysteroscopy allows the inside of the uterus and the openings of the fallopian tubes to be viewed on a video camera or a monitor. The hysteroscope is a telescope that is inserted to look at the walls of the uterus for signs of disease or other problems (such as an IUD that has slipped out of place). It can be guided to the fallopian tubes to find any obstruction and, in some cases, remove it. Some surgical procedures can also be performed with hysteroscopy. The procedure may be performed in a doctor's office, using local anesthetic.

Laparoscopy

In laparoscopy, a lighted tube with a magnifying lens on the end allows the operator to see inside the body. Laparoscopy can be used to diagnose a condition such as endometriosis; it also can be used to perform surgery.

Laparoscopic surgery uses small holes or punctures rather than one large incision. These small incisions result in less postoperative pain and shorter recovery, as compared with an abdominal incision. Women usually return to work within 3 or 4 days after laparoscopy in comparison to 4 to 6 weeks after more extensive surgery.

Many procedures can now be done through a laparoscope:

- Hysterectomy
- Removal of the gallbladder
- Removal of segments of colon

- Assisting vaginal hysterectomy
- Removal of fibroids
- Removal of the fallopian tubes
- Sterilization
- Removal of ovarian cysts

Laser

Laser therapy uses a beam of very intense and focused light to perform surgery. It is used to remove abnormal tissue from the cervix that could be a sign of early cancer. The laser also can remove warts that result from HPV infection. To increase the likelihood of complete cure, a small margin of normal tissue may also be removed. An anesthetic is given before surgery, and recovery is usually very rapid.

Loop Electrosurgical Excision Procedure

For a loop electrosurgical excision procedure, known as LEEP, a high-intensity electrical current passes through a wire used to cut a thin slice of tissue from the cervix. This tissue can be examined under a microscope. In addition to obtaining samples of tissue for diagnosis, LEEP also can be used for treatment by removing abnormal tissue. A local anesthetic is administered before the procedure, and pain medication may be given to ease postoperative discomfort. A minimal discharge is experienced after this procedure.

Ultrasound

In ultrasound, inaudible super-swift sound waves are projected into the body. The reflected echoes are captured to create an image of the internal structures of the body; this is transferred to a black and white image on a monitor screen. From this image the physician or diagnostic expert can tell the size and shape of the ovaries, the uterus, and other pelvic structures. It can determine the age and exact location of the fetus within the uterus. In some situations physical details of a fetus can be identified; it is especially helpful in confirming a possible multiple birth.

CONDITIONS AND DISORDERS IN MEN

When there is a disorder in the reproductive system of men, it can affect several functions, including urination and sexual function.

Benign Prostatic Hyperplasia

The prostate gland continues to grow during most of a man's life. It is common for the prostate gland to become enlarged as a man ages. This growth is called benign prostatic hyperplasia, or BPH. Over half of all men over age 60 and about 90 percent of all men in their 70s and 80s have some symptoms of BPH. Symptoms include a weaker urinary stream and a need to urinate more often, especially at night.

Symptoms are caused by pressure from the

STAGES OF PROSTATE CANCER

Stage I	Cancer, confined within the prostate, is not felt or detected but found incidentally after surgery.
Stage II	Cancer, within the prostate, is usually felt on digital rectal exam.
Stage III	Cancer found outside the prostate in adjacent tissues.
Stage IV	Cancer has spread outside the gland and has metastasized to distant tissues.

prostate growth around the urethra, which obstructs the bladder. The bladder cannot fully empty, leaving urine behind. Eventually this can lead to urinary tract infections, bladder or kidney damage, bladder stones, and incontinence. The cause of BPH is not clear, but is dependent on aging and androgens. Although some of the signs of BPH and prostate cancer are similar, having BPH does not seem to increase the chances of getting prostate cancer.

When BPH causes a partial obstruction of the urethra, certain factors can bring on symptoms. Some over-the-counter cold or allergy medicines can prevent the bladder from allowing urine to pass. Other conditions that can bring on urinary retention include alcohol, cold temperatures, or a long period of immobility.

Treatment may not be required in the early stages. If problems develop, however, medical or surgical treatment may be required. Some medications used to treat BPH shrink the prostate cells or relax the smooth muscle of the prostate. The blood pressure drugs terazosin (Hytrin) and doxazosin can be used to relax smooth muscle in the prostate.

Sometimes, surgery to remove the enlarged part of the prostate is recommended. In most cases, surgery is performed through the urethra with a light-transmitting instrument that has an electrical loop at the end to cut tissue. Surgery can also be performed through an open incision. Most men recover completely within 6 weeks. Sexual function may take a while to return but usually is not affected. After surgery, most men experience retrograde ejaculation, in which they achieve orgasm during sex but the semen travels backward to the bladder rather than forward out the penis.

Cancer

Prostate Cancer

One of the most common cancers in the United States, close to 200,000 new cases of prostate cancer are diagnosed each year. The prevalence of prostate cancer increases rapidly with age, reaching about 50 percent in men over 70. The cancer incidence is higher in African-American men than in white men. In the early stages there are no symptoms.

The cancer is usually discovered by digital rectal examination (DRE), in which a hard lump or growth in the prostate gland can be detected before symptoms develop. Tests are then performed to confirm the diagnosis. In addition to imaging studies, blood tests to measure a chemical called prostate-specific antigen (PSA) are performed to detect the high levels that occur in the presence of cancer. Biopsies are done to obtain a piece of tissue for further study and, if cancer cells are present, the stage of disease is determined (see "Stages of Prostate Cancer," page 112).

Treatment can include surgery, radiation therapy, hormone therapy, or a combination of these treatments. Because prostate cancer cells use the male hormones to grow, blocking production of these hormones with gonadotropin androgens and antiandrogens may control the disease. All of these treatments have side effects. The chance of complete cure is good when the disease is detected in its early stages.

Testicular Cancers

Cancer of the testis is the most common type of cancer in men between the ages of 18 and 35. Two to three new cases per 100,000 males occur in the United States each year. White men are four times more likely than African-American men to develop testicular cancer. Seminoma, the most common type of testicular cancer, has a high cure rate when treated early.

Any unusual lump on the testis, or any new lump, even if it is not painful, should be evaluated by a physician. When a tumor is found in one testis, surgical removal is required; the remaining testis maintains the body's normal functions. The loss of both testes results in loss of hormone production, and testosterone therapy will be necessary to maintain sexual function.

Cryptorchidism

Cryptorchidism is also known as hidden testis or undescended testis, because the testis has not reached its normal position in the scrotum. A physician can confirm the absence of the testis by feeling the scrotum, and all young boys should be checked early for this condition. The undescended testis must be removed if it cannot be put in the normal scrotal position, because it carries increased risk of testicular cancer.

Epididymitis

Infection of the epididymis, the coiled tube that transports sperm to the vas deferens, is caused either by STDs, including chlamydia and gonorrhea, or by E. coli bacteria. This condition is easily transmitted and can be very painful. The infecting organism can sometimes be identified in samples of urine. Antibiotics are usually prescribed. Ice packs applied to the scrotum reduce swelling and pain. It is important to distinguish epididymitis from torsion, or twisting, of the testis, which should be treated immediately.

Gynecomastia

Enlargement of the male breasts, know as gynecomastia, can occur on one or both sides. It is usually triggered by an imbalance in the normal ratio of androgen to estrogen in the blood supply—either androgen production is decreased or estrogen levels are increased. Gynecomastia can occur normally in newborns, at adolescence, or with aging. It also can result from several endocrine disorders and some medications; gynecomastia should be evaluated.

Erectile Dysfunction (Impotence)

The inability to have or keep an erection sufficient to permit intercourse or masturbation is called impotence or erectile dysfunction. Nearly every man experiences temporary impotence related to fatigue, stress, or illness. More than 10 million men in the United States are chronically impotent. The problem increases with age; 30 percent of men age 65 have recurrent episodes of impotence.

Many factors can affect the complex interaction of vascular, neurologic, and endocrine systems that allow normal erectile function. Although sexual function and desire may decrease with age, age is not necessarily a cause of impotence. Medication side effects, stress, smoking, and alcoholism can be risk factors. Inadequate testosterone, anxiety, premature ejaculation, and Peyronie's disease are some of the treatable causes of the problem. Diabetes is the most common disease associated with erectile problems.

Treatment requires a medical history and physical examination; this should include an evaluation of testis size, shape, and consistency and palpation of the shaft of the penis. A testosterone level and a nocturnal penile tumescence test can be used to detect whether a man is having an erection at night while he sleeps. If a man is physically able to have an erection, his impotence could be caused by psychological reasons, and he may benefit from counseling.

Some of the methods of treatment include the use of penile or intracavernous injections, vacuum devices, and penile implants. Support groups, changes in lifestyle, or medications can be helpful.

Infertility

Defined as the inability of a couple to conceive after 12 months of unprotected intercourse, infertility is thought to affect 10 to 15 percent of married couples in the United States. Some of the known causes of male infertility include chromosomal abnormalities, loss of germ cells that produce sperm (which can occur during treatment for cancer), deficient hormones, or physical abnormalities. Infertility can be caused by an inadequate number of sperm, or the sperm may be present but not strong enough to penetrate the egg.

A physician's examination should include palpation of the testes and the epididymis to look for possible obstructions that could prevent sperm from traveling out the penis. A rectal examination should be performed to evaluate the prostate and possible abnormalities of the structures involved in ejaculation. Two or more semen analyses should be done. Additional tests may include evaluation of the hormone testosterone. Treatments are directed at the specific causes identified by the couple's history, the physical exams, and testing.

Peyronie's Disease

In Peyronie's disease a firm plaque or growth occurs on the connective tissue of the penis. This plaque can cause pain during an erection and make vaginal penetration difficult. This growth is not malignant and can go away on its own. If it lasts more than 1 year, surgery may be helpful.

Premature Ejaculation

Ejaculation that occurs just before or shortly after penetration of the woman is considered premature. Often associated with problems in a relationship, it may also be due to inadequate control over the ejaculatory process and does not have a physical cause.

In the past, treatment included efforts to decrease anxiety by concentrating on nonsexual fantasies, use of cerebral depressants or sedatives, and distractive maneuvers such as compressing the glans of the penis. To decrease penile sensation, anesthetic ointments were applied, condoms were used, and penile movement in the vagina was minimized. Today it is recognized that this is a psychological problem that requires behavioral therapy. Such therapy is usually successful when both partners participate.

Priapism

Priapism is a prolonged, often painful penile erection that lasts for more than 4 to 6 hours. It is not associated with sexual desire. Causes are often unclear but include leukemia or sickle-cell anemia. Prolonged erections also can result from the use of drugs and injections into the penis to correct erectile problems. The condition must be treated right away by a urologist to prevent permanent damage to the penis.

Prostatitis

An inflammation of the prostate, prostatitis may arise suddenly or be long lasting or recurring. Symptoms include difficulty urinating; pain in the lower back, muscles, joints, or the area between the scrotum and anus; and painful ejaculation. If untreated, prostatitis can cause abscesses, spread of infection, and urinary retention. Prostatitis is diagnosed by a careful digital rectal examination and urinalysis to identify any bacterial infection. When the condition is caused by bacteria, it is treated with antibiotics; hot baths sometimes provide relief from the symptoms.

Retrograde Ejaculation

In retrograde ejaculation, orgasm occurs, but no ejaculate leaves the penis. This condition usually arises after surgery to remove an enlarged prostate, when the muscles around the bladder neck are removed. Instead of being expelled through the penis, sperm enters the urethra near the opening of the bladder and is flushed out with urine. Although a man may be unable to have children without special assisted techniques, he retains his libido, potency, and ability to have an erection and orgasm.

Testicular Failure

Testicular failure is rare. It is caused by chromosomal abnormalities as well as damage to the mature testes due to disease or injury. The loss of sex drive typical with this condition often can be restored through a program of androgen replacement. Fertility cannot be restored.

Varicocele

A swelling in the scrotum caused by enlarged veins, varicocele is common in otherwise healthy men. It is caused by problems with the valves located in the veins leading from the testes. The blockage causes blood to back up, resulting in swelling and infertility. When varicocele causes infertility, surgery is necessary.

PROCEDURES FOR MEN

Nocturnal Penile Tumescence Test

Sleep-associated erections can be monitored with the nocturnal penile tumescence test to evaluate impotence. Normal males have 3 to 5 erections per night's sleep. Both intrapenile injections and the penile tumescence test may be used in a complete diagnostic evaluation.

Semen Analysis

Semen is collected from a male after 2 or more days of abstinence. Ideally, 2 or more samples are taken over a 75- to 90-day period. A normal sperm count is at least 20 million sperm per milliliter. At least 50 per-

cent of the sperm should be moving, with a signifi-
cant number moving rapidly forward, and at least 50
percent of the sperm should appear normal on microscopic examination. This test should be performed as
a part of an infertility evaluation.

Vasectomy

About a half million men in the United States have
vasectomies each year. A vasectomy is a disruption of
the vas deferens. It often is performed through a small
puncture in the scrotum through which the vas (tubes
that carry sperm from the testes to the urethra) are
tied (see Fig. 2.25). No stitching is required, and the
operation takes no more than 10 minutes. Recovery
takes about 1 week. A semen analysis must be done
to make sure the disruption is complete.

Vasectomies are usually reversible. A vasovasec-
tomy is the rejoining of the two ends of the vas; this
procedure has a high success rate, and a pregnancy
rate of up to 60 percent can result.

Health Care Practitioners

Women can receive care for the reproductive system
from any of the following health care professionals:

- Obstetrician-gynecologist: A specialist who has
  completed 4 years of residency beyond medical
  school in the field of women's health. This
  physician may be the woman's primary care
  doctor or may be consulted for problems relating to the female reproductive system. An obste-

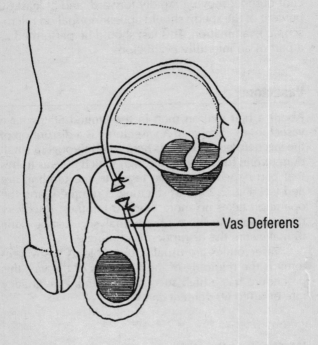

Figure 2.25   Vasectomy
Vasectomy, a form of sterilization for men, is a relatively simple procedure that is very effective for the prevention of pregnancy. A small incision is made in the scrotum, and the vas deferens, the tube through which sperm move from the testes to the urethra, is cut and the ends tied off. Reversal of the procedure has a high success rate.

trician-gynecologist may receive further training for 2 to 3 years in a subspecialty: maternal-fetal medicine (high-risk pregnancy and delivery), reproductive endocrinology (hormone and infertility issues), or gynecologic oncology (cancers of the female reproductive organs). Subspecialists are usually located in major medical centers and see patients on referral.

- Internist: A specialist who has completed at least 3 years of internal medicine training beyond medical school. Some internists do gynecological exams (pelvics and Paps) and some do not.

- Family physician: A physician who has completed at least 3 years of specialty training in family practice beyond medical school. Family physicians routinely do gynecological exams.

- Nurse practitioner: A registered nurse who has received additional training and is licensed to perform certain procedures independently.

- Nurse-midwife: A registered nurse who has additional training in providing obstetric care to women.

For routine examinations, men can see an internal medicine specialist or a family practitioner. A man having a problem with his prostate or infertility may be referred to a urologist for evaluation.

PART III
Sexually Transmitted Diseases

Carol Widrow, M.D.

Sexually transmitted diseases (STDs) are spreading rapidly. Although they are more common now than ever before, many people fail to understand how to protect themselves from contracting an STD. Furthermore, many people do not recognize the early symptoms, or do not know how to get diagnosed and tested for such problems.

Parents often fail to discuss STDs with their children, because they are afraid of talking about sex. The information and education on STDs are limited in some school systems, although these diseases should be fully addressed in junior highs and high schools. The increased sexual promiscuity in the United States over the past 25 years has also helped the STD epidemic grow. Having more than one sexual partner greatly increases the risk of contracting an STD. Although women now have many options for birth control, only the use of condoms, a barrier precaution, greatly reduces the risk of contracting disease.

Some of the most dangerous STDs, including syphilis and gonorrhea, may occur without symptoms. Sexually active persons can carry an STD from one relationship to the next, infecting their new partners, while remaining completely unaware of the presence of disease.

Although most types of STD can be cured with antibiotics, there can be long-term, serious consequences. Many viruses are incurable, and a growing number of STDs can cause infertility in women. The best protection against STDs is to prevent them from occurring and, when they do occur, to obtain treatment immediately.

PREVENTION

The surest way to avoid an STD is to avoid sex. Some women may find abstinence an undesirable option, however. Sexually active women should practice safe sex:

- Limit your sexual partners.
- Know your partner's sexual history.
- Use condoms.

Practicing safe sex means being responsible for yourself as well as your partner. Safe sex can keep you from contracting one of the many types of STDs, including chlamydia, gonorrhea, herpes, syphilis, and genital warts. These types of STD are highly contagious and can be contracted easily. There is no vaccine that can prevent them. Practicing safe sex can also help protect against becoming infected with human immunodeficiency virus (HIV), which causes AIDS (see Part IV).

Other than abstinence, monogamy with an uninfected partner is the best way to avoid picking up an STD. Having several sexual partners greatly increases your risk for STDs. Ask your sexual partners if they have ever had an STD or if they are having sex with others.

Condoms, when used properly, are the most effective method to keep an STD from spreading. A woman should insist that a male sexual partner wear a condom, even if she is using another form of birth control. This is also true for women who do not need birth control, such as those who have gone through menopause or who have had their uterus removed. If a male sexual partner does not want to use a condom, there is now a condom that women can use (see "The Female Condom"). Women must learn to refuse to have sex with a man unless a condom is used.

Condoms are readily available over the counter in most drugstores, and there are many kinds. Condoms made of natural materials do not keep some viruses from passing between you and your partner, so latex condoms should always be used. A spermicide used with a condom may offer additional protection.

You cannot catch most types of STDs from nonsexual contact, such as hugging or holding hands. Most STD organisms cannot survive outside the body for long, so catching an STD from sitting on a toilet seat is very unlikely.

THE FEMALE CONDOM

There is now a condom that women can use themselves rather than relying on their male sex partners. Called the female condom, it consists of two rings with a latex sheath between them. The closed end of the sheath is inserted into the vagina, and the ring is placed high up around the cervix. The open end of the sheath remains outside the uterus. (See Fig. 3.1)

Like the condom for men, female condoms can be bought in drugstores without a prescription. It should be used once and then thrown away. Used as directed, it can be effective in preventing STDs and pregnancy.

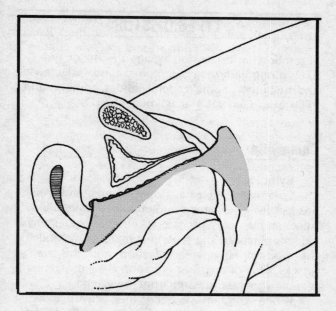

Figure 3.1 Female Condom
The *female condom* is a plastic sheath connected by rings on either end. One ring fits inside the vagina against the cervix (opening of the uterus), and the other ring anchors the sheath outside the body.

In addition to taking steps to prevent getting or passing on an STD, it is important to recognize the symptoms of these diseases. The better a woman understands her body, the better prepared she is to recognize such symptoms.

TYPES OF STDS

The following discussion covers the major types of STDs along with their symptoms, causes, diagnoses, and treatment. Some general guides apply to most STDs (see "General Management of STDs").

Chlamydia

Symptoms

Chlamydia often has no symptoms, and women are less likely to have symptoms than men. Signs of infection may only be noted during a doctor's physical examination. The type of symptoms depends on the type of chlamydia infection and the area it attacks. One of the most common signs in women is a creamy white discharge from the vagina.

When symptoms do occur, they usually appear 1 to 3 weeks after infection. Women usually report a thin vaginal discharge, abdominal pain, and burning during urination. Men often report a burning sensation during urination and a urethral exudate. Men are more likely to display symptoms, women usually learn that they are infected only when their male sexual partner begins to show signs of infection.

Chlamydia commonly results in a genitourinary infection, such as nongonococcal urethritis (NGU), which is marked by a thin penile discharge in men and mild vaginal discharge in women. Chlamydia can infect the cervix (the opening of the uterus), a condition called cervicitis. If the cervicitis is not treated, the infection can move up into the uterus and the fallopian tubes. Infection of the tubes can cause a

GENERAL MANAGEMENT OF STDS

Some guidelines about STDs apply regardless of the type of disease. For the best results, follow these recommendations:

- While taking antibiotics for an STD, complete the recommended treatment, even if symptoms go away before all the antibiotics have been taken. Stopping too soon can allow infection to return and prompt the bacterium or virus to develop resistance to the treatment.

- Sex partners of persons with STDs should be tested and treated. Both partners should be given antibiotics at the same time. This keeps the partners from passing the infection between themselves.

- To prevent reinfection, abstain from intercourse until all antibiotics have been taken and symptoms have diasppeared.

- Use condoms to prevent reinfection.

- Those who have one STD should probably be tested for others. Having one STD puts a person at a risk for others. In particular, gonorrhea and chlamydia commonly occur together. Diseases that cause open sores on the genitals increase the chance of getting AIDS from an infected partner.

dangerous condition called pelvic inflammatory disease (PID), which may result in infertility.

Men and women who have anal sex, can have chlamydia infections of the rectum (proctitis). Swelling and soreness of the lymph nodes and rectal bleeding are signs of infection.

Newborns who get chlamydia from their mothers develop pneumonia and eye infections. Chlamydia is the leading cause of blindness in babies born in developing countries.

Cause
Chlamydia infections are caused by the bacterium *Chlamydia trachomatis*. This infection is the most common STD in the United States, and can be spread through vaginal or anal sex. It often is transmitted along with gonorrhea and contributes to a condition called pelvic inflammatory disease (see "Pelvic Inflammatory Disease," page 137). A woman can pass chlamydia to her baby during its birth. In men chlamydia can cause such manifestations as epididymitis (infection around the testicle) and proctitis.

Diagnosis
Diagnosis of chlamydia is often difficult because it may have no symptoms. A woman may be tested if her partner has been found to be infected. Or she may be tested if she has symptoms, such as vaginitis, or PID.

A sample of discharge can be taken from the vagina or the cervix and tested. A culture is the most accurate way to diagnose chlamydia.

Treatment
The antibiotics recommended for treatment of chlamydia are doxycycline or azithromycin. Doxy-

cycline must be taken for 7 days, but azithromycin—which is newer—can be taken in one dose.

Pregnant women with chlamydia infection are advised to use erythromycin, since tetracycline can adversely affect the fetus.

All sex partners should be informed of the infection. They should be tested if possible, but if testing is not available, they should be treated for chlamydia infection even if they have no symptoms.

Gonorrhea

Symptoms

Both men and women can contract gonorrhea. Women may have no symptoms; however, they usually occur and can include vaginal discharge and dysuria (painful urination). Women may delay treatment because they do not think the discharge is serious.

Men may have no symptoms for a 3- to 6-day period (called the incubation period). At the end of this time, they often develop a tingling sensation in the urethra followed by painful urination and a white discharge. With some strains of gonorrheal bacterium there may never be a discharge.

Symptoms vary, depending on the site infected. Men and women who have anal sex may have rectal discharge and discomfort; men and women who engage in oral sex may experience sore throat, pain on swallowing, enlarged cervical lymph nodes, and red tonsils with a discharge, often confused with strep throat. Women who have infection of the reproductive organs can have severe lower abdominal pain and fever. These signs may be the beginning of PID, a common cause of infertility in women. Infection of the fallopian tubes occurs in nearly 15 percent of the women who contract gonorrhea.

In its advanced stages, gonorrhea can enter the bloodstream and spread throughout the body, causing complications. It can attack the heart and joints, but these developments can be prevented through treatment.

Cause

Gonorrhea is caused by the bacterium *Neisseria gonorrhoeae*. It is second only to chlamydia in terms of number of cases in the United States. About 45 percent of people with gonorrhea also have chlamydia, and the risk factors of infection are similar. Even though the number of cases of gonorrhea seems to be dropping, about 1 million new cases are still reported each year. It is most common in people between the ages of 15 and 30. Babies born to mothers with the disease can contract an infection called gonococcal ophthalmia neonatorum at birth when they pass through the vagina. This condition can affect the baby's eyes, causing blindness, and requires a different antibiotic than that used to treat chlamydia infection in the newborn.

Diagnosis

Gonorrhea is diagnosed from a specimen taken from the infected area. A swab is used to take a sample of discharge from the urethra, cervix, rectum, or throat, depending on which areas were exposed. A sample(s) will be cultured so that every involved area can be definitively diagnosed.

Treatment

Women with gonorrhea as well as their sex partners should be treated. Anyone with gonorrhea should avoid all sexual activity while under treatment, because the disease is very easily spread.

Many types of drugs are used to fight gonorrhea. Although once antibiotics such as penicillin and tetracycline were the mainstays of treatment, today a large percentage of gonorrhea bacteria are resistant to these drugs. Therefore, newer drugs like ceftriaxone are used. Because gonorrhea and chlamydia often occur together, doctors usually recommend that patients also take doxycycline to eliminate any undiagnosed chlamydia.

Pregnant women can be safely treated with ceftriaxone. In case they also have a chlamydial infection, they are usually treated with erythromycin as well.

In women with simple infections whose symptoms are cleared by treatment, further testing is not needed. However, women who continue to have symptoms should be tested to see if the bacterium persists, and if so, what types of antibiotics are likely to eliminate it.

Genital Warts

Symptoms

Genital warts begin as tiny red or pink bumps. After about 2 months (the incubation period can range from 1 to 6 months), they become moist on the surface. The warts will spread if left untreated. In males they are usually located on the scrotum or on the shaft or tip of the penis. In women they grow on the vulva, on the cervical and vaginal walls, and around the anus. The virus can also cause growths on the cervix.

Cause
Also called venereal warts or condyloma, genital warts are caused by the human papillomavirus (HPV). This virus causes warts on the skin of men and women and is easily transmitted by sexual contact. There are many different types of HPV that can cause warts. Some types have been linked to a risk of cervical cancer. (See Part II).

Diagnosis
Genital warts look similar to typical skin warts. A trained eye often can diagnose genital warts without any tests. Painting the area with a weak acid solution causes the warts to turn white, which can help in diagnosis. Warts on the cervix can be detected by a Pap test, in which a sample of cells is removed from the cervix for study under a microscope. A sample of the wart can be taken and studied to reveal what type of HPV is causing the infection.

Treatment
Genital warts are treated by removing the warts from both partners. Medications that are placed on the wart include a natural resin called podofilox (which inhibits wart growth) and acids such as trichloroacetic or bichloroacetic acid (which dry up the warts). Podofilox should not be used by pregnant women.

Other options include laser surgery and freezing the warts, called cryotherapy. Electrodesiccation (sending an electrical current through the tissue, which then dries up) is also used to remove the warts.

Although the visible warts can be removed, this does not cure the virus. As yet there is no cure or vaccine for HPV. Since the virus may remain in the body, warts may come back and require further treatment. Because of the risk of cancer, women who contract the virus should have frequent and regular Pap tests.

PELVIC INFLAMMATORY DISEASE

When an STD moves from the vulva and vagina up to the uterus and fallopian tubes, it causes pelvic inflammatory disease (PID). PID can cause infertility in a woman even without symptoms.

Most cases of PID occur when *Chlamydia trachomatis* or *Neisseria gonorrhoeae* spreads up the fallopian tubes, but they can be caused by other STDs as well.

The use of an intrauterine device (IUD) for birth control can increase the risk of PID, with the greatest risk coming a few months after the IUD is inserted. Women who develop PID after using an IUD are usually advised to have it removed.

A woman may have no symptoms of PID until its advanced stages. Then, it can cause abdominal and low back pain and fever. White blood cells, working to eliminate the infection, may cause a discharge.

PID is one of the major preventable causes of infertility in women. The infection in the fallopian tubes can cause abscesses and scar tissue to form in the tubes that may block sperm from passing through them, leaving the woman infertile. Approximately 13 percent of women who have 1 attack of PID are left infertile. Those who suffer 3 attacks of PID have a 75 percent chance of becoming infertile.

PID is diagnosed during a gynecological exam and lab testing for STDs. Although chlamydia and gonorrhea are commonly diagnosed as the causes of PID, these two types of organisms can die quickly. They may not be easily cultured at the time testing is done. The common bacterium *Escherichia coli,* found in the digestive and genital tracts of healthy women, is often the only type of bacterium noted at the time of the diagnosis.

PID is treated with antibiotics that may be administered orally or intravenously, depending on the severity of the infection. In some cases, surgery is required to remove abscesses that remain after antibiotic treatment.

Genital Herpes

Symptoms

The symptoms of genital herpes first appear after a 3- to 7-day incubation period. Genital herpes is characterized by pain and itching in the genital area along with blisters or open sores. When these are present, a person is said to be having an outbreak. The first outbreak of genital herpes is usually marked by additional flulike symptoms, including fever, headache, and swollen lymph nodes in the groin area. Recurrent outbreaks tend to have more localized symptoms.

The symptoms are usually preceded by a tingly or burning sensation in the area, that will later develop into tiny red blisters in both men and women. These blisters then grow into larger pimplelike bumps that have a watery yellow center. The blisters rupture, and within 3 or 4 days a crust forms.

In both sexes, the blisters can appear in the genital area and on the thighs, abdomen, buttocks, and anus. In women, blisters usually appear on the labia and around the clitoris. In men, they may appear on the penis and scrotum. Sometimes blisters near the opening of the urethra and on the tip of the penis will swell up, making urination difficult and painful.

Blisters may also develop internally on the female cervix and vaginal walls or inside the male urethra. These internal lesions may make it difficult for men to urinate and difficult to detect the virus in women.

The entire process of a herpes outbreak, from initial tingle to dried-up crust, can last about 3 weeks, but the virus may still be active—and the infected person contagious—for 2 weeks after the symptoms disappear. Although the virus is most contagious during the blistering stage, it can be transmitted during the early phase of burning and tingling as well.

Even though the symptoms subside, the virus moves to the nerve cells in the base of the spinal cord, where it is dormant. During a recurrent outbreak, the virus travels down the nerves to the genital area and causes a new set of blisters and more distress. Between 50 and 75 percent of those who have an initial outbreak will suffer a recurrent infection within 3 months. The cause of the recurrent attacks is unknown, but there does seem to be a correlation between outbreaks and stress or a weakened immune system.

There is no cure for genital herpes, but each successive outbreak has fewer and weaker symptoms. After a number of years, the outbreaks may disappear.

If a pregnant woman has open herpes lesions, she runs the risk of infecting her baby as it passes through the vagina at birth. If infected, the baby may suffer brain damage, blindness, or death if not treated. A pregnant woman with herpes will be examined when she is in labor. If she has active sores, she should have her baby by cesarean section.

Cause

About 150 million people in the United States are thought to have been exposed to herpes simplex virus, the virus that causes genital herpes. Each year, about 300,000 new cases are diagnosed. Herpes simplex virus type 2 causes about 80 percent of cases of genital herpes. The other 20 percent is caused by herpes simplex type 1 virus, better known as the cause of sores on the mouth and lips.

The virus is transmitted through sexual contact—vaginal, anal, or oral—and can also enter the body through mucous membranes or cuts in the skin. Genital herpes can also infect the eyes if fingers carrying the virus touch the eyes. Active genital herpes is highly contagious. Transmission is known to occur during inapparent activation of the infection, even when blisters or open sores are not visible.

Diagnosis

A diagnosis of genital herpes is made by taking a sample culture from a liquid-filled blister or a sore in its early phase.

Treatment

Genital herpes has no cure but a vaccine for prevention is being developed. Keeping the infected area clean and dry can help improve a person's comfort when having an outbreak. Use of the oral drug acyclovir can reduce the length of time the virus can be transmitted, shorten the healing time, and decrease the severity of symptoms. Pregnant women are best served by using the topical form. Persons who have frequent recurrences can take acyclovir daily to prevent attacks. Because the infection is usually contracted while sores are present, abstaining from sex until sores are completely healed can help stop the spread of herpes. Transmission, however, can occur during active disease without blisters or symptoms; therefore the safest approach is to use a condom.

Syphilis

Symptoms

Syphilis occurs in three stages: primary, secondary, and tertiary. The signs of primary syphilis are painless sores called chancres on the genitals, tongue, lips, breast, or rectum, along with swollen lymph nodes in the adjacent area. If the sore is located in a woman's vagina, it can easily go undetected. The incubation period for primary syphilis is 2 to 3 weeks and sometimes as long as 8 weeks.

Secondary syphilis begins in 2 to 6 weeks after the chancre heals, usually without treatment. The signs of secondary syphilis may include fever, headache, aching joints, and a skin rash. The skin rash appears diffusely as well as on the bottoms of feet and the palms of hands.

An infected person then can go through a period when syphilis is latent, that is without signs or symptoms. That may be followed by tertiary syphilis if the person is not treated. Latent syphilis can be life threatening because the bacteria by this time have spread throughout the body and into the blood system and brain. Tertiary syphilis, which appears years later, can cause a number of problems, including nerve and brain damage and heart disease. These severe symptoms are not very common in the United States, since syphilis rarely progresses to this late stage.

Women infected with syphilis can pass the infection to their unborn fetus during pregnancy. About 50 percent of those fetuses infected will be born prematurely or stillborn. Those infants that do survive may appear healthy at birth but develop problems later.

Cause

Until the recent arrival of acquired immunodeficiency syndrome (AIDS), syphilis was the most serious of the STDs. It is caused by the bacterium *Treponema pallidum*. Although it was once a very common infection, today syphilis is rarer than chlamydia and gonorrhea. In the past few years, however, the incidence of syphilis has increased, especially within the homosexual community.

Syphilis is contracted during sexual contact, through cuts or sores in the skin or mucous membranes. The disease is very contagious. It can also pass through the blood and to an unborn fetus from an infected mother.

Diagnosis

Infection is suspected based on the presence of sores (for primary syphilis) or rash and flulike symptoms (for secondary syphilis). A positive blood test is necessary to diagnose syphilis. Even if a person has no symptoms, a blood test can usually detect syphilis.

Some states require syphilis tests before issuing marriage licenses, so some people learn only then that they have syphilis at that time. Others are tested for syphilis when they enter a hospital. Because of the danger of syphilis for the fetus, all pregnant women are tested for syphilis.

Treatment

Penicillin given intramuscularly is effective for primary and secondary syphilis. Latent syphilis can also be treated with penicillin to prevent complications, but must be given longer and at higher doses to achieve success during this phase. Penicillin can be used safely to treat pregnant women and prevent transmission to their fetus. It can also be used to treat infected infants. Penicillin is the most commonly used antibiotic for syphilis, but doxycycline or tetracycline can be used for those who are allergic to penicillin.

Because syphilis can be spread when open lesions are present, sexual contact of any kind should be avoided during this time. Routine blood tests are required for one year following the initial syphilis infection to determine whether treatment has been successful.

Trichomonas

Symptoms

Common symptoms in women include an abundant yellow frothy musty-smelling discharge. Sores may form on the cervix. The vulva may itch, and urinating may be painful. Most men with trichomonas infection do not have symptoms.

Trichomonas infection is caused by a small organism called *Trichomonas vaginalis*. It affects about 15 percent of sexually active women and 10 percent of sexually active men. It causes symptoms like those of vaginitis (see Part II). Because the organism can live outside the vagina, nonsexual transmission may also occur.

Diagnosis
To diagnose trichomonas infection, a sample of the discharge is taken and examined under a microscope.

Treatment
Trichomonas infection is not usually serious and can be treated easily with metronidazole. Usually just one dose is needed, but some doctors choose to give a lower dose for 7 days. A woman and her sex partner(s) must be treated. They should avoid having sex until they have completed their treatment and no longer have symptoms. Anyone who is taking metronidazole should avoid drinking alcohol, which can cause severe nausea and vomiting when mixed with metronidazole.

Cytomegalovirus

Symptoms
CMV often has no symptoms. Women who do have symptoms may have a mild illness similar to the flu. Although CMV is not harmful for most women, it causes special concerns for a pregnant woman, who can pass CMV to her fetus through the umbilical cord. CMV is most risky if a woman first becomes infected while she is pregnant. If this happens, the

fetus can be harmed. CMV can also be passed to the infant during birth and later through breast milk. Approximately 50 percent of mothers who have CMV pass it on to their infants, and of those infants, 5 to 15 percent will have abnormal central nervous systems at birth.

Cause
Cytomegalovirus (CMV) is caused by a virus with the same name. Up to 70 percent of people have evidence in their blood that they have been infected with CMV. Children can contract the disease from an infected mother. One of the most common ways a woman gets CMV is by being exposed to children, for example, in day care. CMV also may be passed on through blood transfusions or through sexual activity with an infected partner.

Diagnosis
Cytomegalovirus is diagnosed through a blood test for CMV antibodies. Infection in the fetus can be diagnosed by testing blood or the amniotic fluid.

Treatment
There is no cure for CMV. Because a fetus can develop severe abnormalities if infected with the virus early in development, tests are performed early in pregnancy. Infection of the fetus late in pregnancy may lead to childhood hearing and learning problems.

Chancroid

Symptoms
The initial symptom is one or more painful swellings (boils) that appear in the genital area. If ignored, these lesions will rupture and release pus.

Cause
Rare in the United States but common in the tropics, chancroid is caused by the organism *Haemophilus ducreyi,* which is passed during sex across genital mucous membranes. It moves through the lymphatic system into the groin area to infect the glands.

Diagnosis
A microscopic examination of the pus is necessary to determine the cause of any lesions. Syphilis has similar symptoms, so this examination will rule out syphilis.

Treatment
Azithromycin, ceftriaxone, or erythromycin is most commonly given to treat the patient and prevent spread of the disease. Gentle pressure on lesions can also help accelerate their healing. Even if they don't have symptoms, sex partners of women with chancroid should also be examined and treated.

PART IV
AIDS and Women

Carol Widrow, M.D.

Infection with human immunodeficiency virus (HIV) leads to a condition called acquired immune deficiency syndrome (AIDS). The infection causes the body's immune system, which fights disease, to weaken, leaving it open to a range of other diseases. It can take 8 to 10 years from the initial infection with HIV to the development of symptoms of full-blown AIDS. During that time, a person with HIV can pass the virus to others. The infection is transmitted through sex, exposure to blood or blood products of individuals who are infected, and from a mother who is HIV positive to her infant. Although treatment is available to help limit the progression of the conditions that occur with AIDS, there is no cure.

Since its discovery in 1982, AIDS has reached epidemic proportions throughout the world. The World Health Organization, which is devoted to promoting better health internationally, estimates that 13 million men, women, and children worldwide are infected with HIV. In the United States, 1 million individuals are estimated to be infected with HIV. More than 400,000 individuals have AIDS, and over 245,000 have died from it according to the Centers for Disease Control and Prevention (CDC), a federal agency that monitors the disease and issues guidelines for its management.

In the U.S., infection with HIV affects all groups, although it occurs in minority populations more than it does in white populations. Through 1992, 47 percent of all reported AIDS cases were among African-Americans and Hispanics, although these two groups represent only 21 percent of the total population. Although the disease was originally prevalent mostly in homosexual men, heterosexual sex is now the most common mode of infection worldwide and is the fastest growing mode of transmission in the United States. The increase in heterosexual transmission has led to a dramatic increase in HIV infection in women, who comprised almost 13 percent of the AIDS cases diagnosed in 1992. In the U.S., AIDS is the fourth leading cause of death in women of reproductive age and the leading cause of death in black women of reproductive age.

AIDS is also among the top 10 causes of death for children aged 1 to 4 years. Infants of mothers who are HIV infected have a 15 to 30 percent risk of acquiring the virus and will also become motherless as a result of AIDS.

As can be seen, HIV infection and AIDS are enormous public health issues. In the absence of an effective vaccine, the best way to bring the spread of HIV under control is through prevention. This can be done by avoiding practices that pose a risk for transmitting the virus.

HOW HIV IS TRANSMITTED

HIV can be found in the body fluids of an infected individual. These fluids include blood as well as semen, saliva, vaginal secretions, amniotic fluid (which surrounds the fetus in the mother's uterus during pregnancy), breast milk, and urine. It is transmitted three ways:

1. Exposure during sexual activity to body secretions of individuals who are infected.
2. Exposure to blood or blood products, such as

TABLE 4.1 AIDS AMONG WOMEN

Age at diagnosis (years)	White, not Hispanic		Black, not Hispanic		Hispanic		Asian/Pacific Islander		American Indian/ Alaska Native		Total	
	No.	(%)	No.	(%)	No.	(%)	No.	(%)	No.	(%)	No.	(%)
Under 5	360	(3)	1,362	(5)	535	(5)	6	(2)	7	(5)	2,277	(4)
5-12	101	(1)	230	(1)	127	(1)	6	(2)	–	–	466	(1)
13-19	113	(1)	358	(1)	91	(1)	1	(0)	1	(1)	565	(1)
20-24	802	(6)	1,737	(6)	751	(7)	15	(5)	16	(11)	3,325	(6)
25-29	2,316	(18)	4,786	(16)	2,053	(18)	27	(10)	29	(20)	9,222	(17)
30-34	2,970	(23)	6,975	(24)	2,746	(25)	56	(20)	38	(26)	12,806	(24)
35-39	2,381	(18)	6,377	(22)	2,150	(19)	45	(16)	21	(14)	10,995	(20)
40-44	1,403	(11)	3,804	(13)	1,289	(12)	42	(15)	14	(10)	6,561	(12)
45-49	765	(6)	1,614	(6)	627	(6)	25	(9)	8	(6)	3,044	(6)
50-54	444	(3)	878	(3)	362	(3)	15	(5)	3	(2)	1,705	(3)
55-59	380	(3)	504	(2)	219	(2)	10	(4)	4	(3)	1,119	(2)
60-64	295	(2)	320	(1)	112	(1)	13	(5)	3	(2)	743	(1)
65 or older	685	(5)	328	(1)	118	(1)	16	(6)	1	(1)	1,149	(2)
Total	13,015	(100)	29,273	(100)	11,181	(100)	277	(100)	145	(100)	53,978	(100)
	198,130		130,384		68,903		2,706		944		401,749	

Source: U.S. Department of Health and Human Services, Public Health Service, CDC, Atlanta, GA 30333.

TABLE 4.2 WAYS WOMEN GET AIDS

Exposure category	White, not Latino No.	(%)	African-American, not Latino No.	(%)	Latino No.	(%)	Asian/Pacific Islander No.	(%)	American Indian/Alaska Native No.	(%)	Totals No.	(%)
Injecting drug use	5,426	(43)	14,160	(51)	4,923	(47)	43	(16)	65	(47)	24,660	(48)
Hemophilia/coagulation disorder	56	(0)	20	(0)	6	(0)	1	(0)	–	–	83	(0)
Heterosexual contact:	4,536	(36)	9,014	(33)	4,479	(43)	118	(45)	46	(33)	18,217	(36)
Sex with injecting drug user	2,131		4,968		2,798		35		30		9,976	
Sex with bisexual male	766		576		220		34		3		1,601	
Sex with person with hemophilia	168		26		14		2		2		212	
Sex with transfusion recipient with HIV infection	203		79		67		12		–		363	
Sex with HIV-infected person, risk not specified	1,268		3,365		1,380		35		11		6,065	
Receipt of blood transfusion, blood components, or tissue	1,489	(12)	725	(3)	389	(4)	62	(23)	10	(7)	2,676	(5)
Risk not reported or identified	1,047	(8)	3,762	(14)	722	(7)	41	(15)	17	(12)	5,599	(11)
Total	12,544	(100)	27,681	(100)	10,519	(100)	265	(100)	138	(100)	51,235	(100)

Source: U.S. HIV and AIDS Cases Reported through June 1994, U.S. Department of Health and Human Services, Public Health Service, CDC, Atlanta, GA 30333.

    through a transfusion or when sharing needles with other intravenous drug using individuals.
3. During pregnancy, when a mother who is infected can pass the virus to her fetus, or during delivery or breast-feeding.

The virus is not spread through casual contact. It is not transmitted through sharing food and drink; touching everyday objects such as linens, telephones, doorknobs, and toilet seats; using swimming pools or hot tubs; hugging or casual kissing; coughing or sneezing; being exposed to another person's tears or sweat; getting bitten by an insect. (See Table 4.2)

Sexual Activity

Women are at greater risk than men during heterosexual sex, because the virus seems to be much more easily transmitted from men to women than from women to men. Any interruption or break in the skin or mucous membranes of the genital tract (the vagina, penis, and anus) increases access of the virus via infected semen, blood, or vaginal secretions. These interruptions can occur through traumatic sex, which causes tearing of the skin or lining of the genital tract, or through sores that occur with sexually transmitted diseases such as herpes or syphilis. Types of intercourse that have a high risk of trauma, such as anal intercourse, also have a high risk of infection with HIV. Bisexual men who engage in this activity also have sexual contact with women, who can then acquire the infection.

    Lesbians appear to be at much less of a risk of contracting the virus from sexual contact, provided they know the risk factors of their partners. Most women with HIV who have had sexual contact only with other women have a history of intravenous drug use or have received blood products. There is a slight risk of transmitting the virus through sexual intercourse during menstruation when one partner is HIV positive and through practices such as digital manipulation or sharing of mechanical devices. In general, when one partner of a lesbian couple is infected, there is a real but low risk that the virus can be transmitted to the uninfected partner.

Exposure to Blood and Blood Products

Intravenous drug use is a major cause of HIV infection. If needles are shared, small amounts of contaminated blood can transmit the virus from one person to another. An infected intravenous drug user also can transmit the virus to sex partners. More than 50 percent of the women who have contracted AIDS from heterosexual transmission had a sex partner who was an intravenous drug user. In addition, many of these women are themselves intravenous drug users. Women who are HIV positive can transmit the virus to their children. Over 70 percent of children with AIDS have mothers who are intravenous drug users or mothers who are sexual partners of intravenous drug users.

Before 1985, blood donated to blood banks was not tested for HIV, so people who received blood transfusions were at risk for infection. Since then, all donated blood has been tested for HIV, and the blood donors are screened for their risk of transmitting the virus. The blood supply is now considered to be quite safe (99 percent).

Individuals with blood disorders, especially those with hemophilia, depend on donated blood to obtain clotting factors, which control bleeding. Clotting factors are produced in blood products derived from blood donations. Since 1985, clotting factors have been heated, inactivating HIV and making the blood products generally safe.

Health care workers are also at risk of being exposed to the blood of an infected individual during emergency and routine medical procedures. Surgery and dental work can result in accidental exposure to HIV. All health care workers are advised to follow what are called *universal precautions,* a set of guidelines established by the CDC to protect them from exposure to HIV and other viruses.

Pregnancy

A woman who is HIV positive has about a 1 in 3 chance of infecting her child with the virus. During pregnancy, viruses may cross the placenta (which passes nourishment to the fetus from the mother) and infect the fetus. The newborn may become infected by exposure to the mother's blood and vaginal secretions during birth. Breast-feeding can cause infection, especially in mothers who contracted HIV shortly after the baby's birth. Therefore, it is recommended that women who are infected do not breast-feed their infants.

It is difficult to tell at the time of birth if a child is infected, because the mother's antibodies (part of the immune system) are present in the newborn's blood. Thus all infants born to women who are HIV positive have HIV antibodies in their blood. If the child is *not* infected, he or she will test HIV negative by the age of 15 to 18 months, when the mother's antibodies have been replaced by the infant's own. An 18-month-old child who tests positive, however, is almost certainly infected. Children who are infected usually have symptoms within the first 3 years of life, although some do not develop signs of AIDS for 7 or more years. In general, the course of disease and survival rates are worse for children who show signs of the disease within the first year of life.

Because HIV can be spread through semen, women who undergo artificial insemination, in which semen from a donor is placed into the cervical area, can be infected with HIV in this way. Not all sperm banks screen donors for HIV, so there is a risk of infection. It is imperative for a recipient to ascertain if donors are screened before they accept semen.

TESTING FOR HIV

A person can be tested to determine whether HIV infection has occurred. The test detects antibodies in the blood. Antibodies are proteins produced in response to a foreign protein of the virus. Once a person is infected, the body begins to produce antibodies, which can be detected in the blood 6 to 12 weeks after infection. These early weeks are called the *window period,* which is the time when a person is infected but an antibody test is negative.

Two tests are used to detect HIV. The first test is an enzyme-linked immunosorbent assay, usually referred to as ELISA. It is used as a screening test, which may be repeated if the test is positive. The second test is called a Western blot, which is used to confirm the positive results of the ELISA test. Both tests detect antibodies to HIV in the blood, but the Western blot is more specific than the ELISA test.

Although these tests are over 99 percent accurate, false-positive results (showing the infection is present when it isn't) and false-negative results (showing the infection is not present when it is) can occur. One of the reasons for false results is the period between the time when a person becomes infected and when antibodies appear. If a person is tested soon after infection, antibodies may not yet have been produced to show up on the test.

Some doctors suggest that everyone be tested for HIV, regardless of individual risk. Anyone who is exposed to risk factors should be tested for HIV. Testing is also recommended if a person shows signs of HIV infection. Because the virus can be passed from mother to baby, a woman who is pregnant or considering pregnancy may wish to be tested, since new information shows treatment can significantly reduce the baby's risk. If there is a question about a sex partner's history, the testing is worth considering. Many women who test positive for HIV do not have a history of any risk factors except having had sex with a man, which confirms the importance of the heterosexual route of transmission.

If you choose to have an HIV test, be sure to receive counseling before the test and after the results are provided. Counseling should include information about risk behaviors and how to change them. It also should explain how to get special health care and how to avoid passing the virus to others, if the tests are positive. If test results are positive, you should take steps to ensure your health as well as the health of others with whom you may come in contact. Because of potential discrimination against individuals who are HIV positive, conveying results of tests is strictly confidential, except as provided by law in certain states.

PREVENTION OF HIV INFECTION

As the number of people infected with HIV increases, individual risk of contracting the virus also increases. This is a fatal disease and has no cure, so the best protection is through prevention: practicing safe sex, avoiding intravenous drug use, ensuring the safety of blood products, and having a healthy pregnancy.

Practicing Safe Sex

Safe sex practices can lower your risk of HIV infection. These practices involve limiting the number of your sex partners, knowing the history of your sex partners, always using a condom, and avoiding certain practices that could cause trauma.

The history of a sex partner can also pose a risk. If you have sex with someone who has had sex with someone who has risk factors, there is a possibility that you could be infected with HIV. It is best to question sexual partners about their history: Ask whether they have ever used intravenous drugs or had sex with someone who did and ask about other sex partners or bisexual practices. Always ask your partners to use a condom, and if they refuse, limit your sexual activities to touching, kissing, or other forms of sexual expression that do not involve intercourse.

Condoms should always be used during sexual intercourse. It is important that condoms be used consistently and properly—most condom failure is the result of incorrect use. Condoms not only prevent pregnancy but also offer protection against sexually transmitted diseases such as herpes, syphilis, and chlamydia as well as AIDS. Although condoms cannot totally eliminate the risk of transmission of HIV, if used correctly, they decrease the risk of infection by eliminating your contact with semen and any penile lesions your partner may have.

Latex condoms provide better protection than natural membrane condoms, which although they appear intact can have pores through which the virus can pass. If lubricant is required with condom use, use only water-based lubricants, because oil- or petroleum-based lubricants can weaken the latex and allow the virus to pass through. Condoms should be used with the spermicide nonoxynol-9. Spermicide use increases the contraceptive effectiveness rate of the condom as well as helps kill HIV. Oral contraceptives, diaphragms, and intrauterine devices are all good methods of birth control, but they do not offer any protection against HIV or sexually transmitted diseases. Always supplement these methods with the use of condoms.

When you become involved in a mutually faithful relationship, you will want to know when you can stop using condoms. Before condom use is discontinued, it is advisable that both you and your partner be tested for HIV 3 to 6 months after either of you has had sexual contact with a different partner.

Specific sexual practices can also increase your

risk of HIV infection. There is a great likelihood of
trauma with anal sex, and the virus is easily absorbed
into the bloodstream through the rectum. Condoms
are also likely to break during anal sex. HIV can also
spread through oral sex, especially if there are
cuts, tears, or sores in the mouth. For oral sex with a
man, condoms should be used. For oral sex with a
woman, a condom cut open, plastic wrap, or a dental dam (a square of latex used for oral surgery)
should be used. If a sexual device (dildo or vibrator)
is shared, it should be disinfected with bleach or rubbing alcohol every time it is used. Some type of pro-

RISK FACTORS

The following factors, whether they apply to
an individual or to an individual's sex partner,
increase the risk of infection with HIV:

- Injecting drugs, especially with shared
  needles

- Current or past sexual contact with

  More than one partner

  Someone who has tested positive for
  HIV or who has AIDS

  A man who has had sex with another
  man, whether he is mainly heterosexual,
  bisexual, or homosexual

- Receiving blood or blood products before
  1985

- Current or past sexually transmitted diseases such as gonorrhea, chlamydia,
  syphilis, or hepatitis B

tection should be used if there is a risk that sex acts may draw blood or tear skin.

Avoiding Drug Use

About 50 percent of the women who test positive for HIV are infected through intravenous drug use. If needles are shared, HIV-infected blood left in needles after injecting drugs can infect the next person who uses the needle.

If you do use drugs, never share needles or any of the equipment used to inject drugs. All equipment should be sterilized. Needles can be sterilized by flushing twice with pure laundry bleach. Bleach should be removed by flushing twice with tap water. Because of the risk of HIV infection with intravenous drug use, many municipalities are distributing clean needles to drug-addicted individuals as a means of controlling the spread of AIDS.

Ensuring the Safety of Blood Products

Since 1985, the risk of HIV infection through blood transfusion has been low. A slight risk does exist, however. One of the ways to avoid infection by blood transfusion is to donate your own blood before any planned surgery so that, if blood is needed, your own blood can be used. Health care workers should follow the universal precautions, which include wearing masks, gloves, and protective clothing during certain medical procedures as protection against exposure to infected blood.

Having a Healthy Pregnancy

Sperm can transmit HIV. Thus a woman who is trying to become pregnant may become infected. The best way to protect yourself against infection is for both

---

A DIALOGUE ABOUT AIDS

Talking with partners about the risk of AIDS is key to a healthy relationship. AIDS can be a difficult thing to talk about, but it can be deadly not to discuss it. Here are some points for women to raise:

- Have you ever had sex with a man?
- Have you ever used drugs? Do you use drugs now?
- Have you ever had a sex partner who was a drug user?
- How many sex partners have you had in the past year?

If the answers aren't reassuring or if your partner will not consent to the use of a condom, set limits and tell your partner about your decisions. Your partner should accept your choices; if not, it may be better to stop having sex for a time than to risk your health. If your partner becomes abusive because of your choice to have safe sex, this is a sign that the relationship is not a healthy one between adults who care about each other. Exercise good judgment: People are not always exactly truthful when they want to have sex with someone.

---

you and your partner to be tested for HIV before having unprotected sex.

If you choose to become pregnant by artificial insemination, that is, by having semen inserted into your cervix, the donor should be tested before his sperm is used.

If you are pregnant and HIV positive, you have a risk of passing the virus to your fetus during pregnancy. Preliminary studies show that this risk can be reduced by 66 percent by getting treatment during pregnancy. Treatment is most effective when it is given to women who do not have advanced disease. HIV infection and AIDS do not seem to have an effect on the pregnancy itself. Because of the risk to the fetus, however, if you are infected with HIV or at risk of being infected, you should seek special prenatal care.

THE AIDS PROCESS

HIV infection means that the virus has entered the bloodstream and has begun to break down the immune system. The immune system helps protect your body from viruses, bacteria, parasites, and fungi. If any infection occurs, special white blood cells, called T cells, are activated to defend your body against the infection.

HIV infects T cells that have a specific surface protein called CD4. HIV binds to the CD4 protein on the white blood cell, thus beginning the course of infection. Once attached, the virus enters the cell and multiplies, eventually killing the T cell. As more and more of the T cells die, the body's ability to fight certain types of infections weakens. This leaves a person who is HIV positive open to so-called opportunistic infections. Such infections are able to take hold because of the person's weakened immune system.

A person with HIV infection may remain healthy for many years. It can take 8 to 10 years or even longer after the initial infection with HIV until serious illness and infections appear. These illnesses tend to occur after HIV has left few T cells alive. Until then, a person with HIV may show signs of certain types of infection that come and go, as their immune system starts to weaken.

The Initial Infection

Once HIV infects the cells, 40 to 60 percent of individuals will develop antibodies to the virus within about 1 to 8 weeks after exposure. Symptoms similar to flu or mononucleosis occur, including fever (with or without swollen glands), rash, sore throat, fatigue, muscle aches, nausea, vomiting, and/or diarrhea. These symptoms last between 3 and 14 days. After recovery from the primary infection, the individual who is HIV positive usually has no symptoms for some time. The virus is being shed or passed into body fluids, however, and can be passed to others. Antibodies to HIV develop in almost all individuals who are infected within 2 to 3 months.

Early Markers of HIV Infection

As the immune system decreases in efficiency, individuals who are HIV-infected begin to show signs of HIV disease. Early signs of immune system deficiency include generalized lymphadenopathy—a persistent swelling of the lymph glands—as well as fever, night sweats, diarrhea, weight loss, and fatigue. These signs occur in both men and women. Effects specific to women have not been fully studied, but those that have been observed often appear as routine gynecologic problems. Their presence should alert both women and their physicians to the possibility of HIV infection in those who otherwise may not have risk factors. Some early markers of HIV infection in women include the following conditions.

Recurrent Vaginal Candidiasis

Candidiasis is commonly known as a yeast infection, which women often get when they take antibiotics, are pregnant, or have diabetes. The symptoms are a thick white or yellow discharge, vaginal itch or burning, and pain when urinating. Such infections may be HIV related when they occur more than 3 times in a 6-month period or are difficult to treat. HIV infection may be suspected if no other cause for yeast infection can be identified.

Cervical Disease

It is unclear if cervical intraepithelial neoplasia (CIN), a precancerous lesion on the opening of the uterus, occurs more often in women with HIV. It is clear, however, that when CIN occurs in women infected with HIV it is more advanced, persistent, and difficult to treat, and it recurs more often than in women who are not infected with HIV. There are a number of risk factors besides HIV infection that are related to CIN. Women with more advanced CIN, however, may wish to be tested for HIV. CIN can lead to invasive cancer, which can be prevented if cervical disease is detected in its early stages. All women should have a Pap test yearly to screen for cervical disease. Women with HIV should consider having a pelvic exam every 6 months.

Herpes and Human Papillomavirus

Certain viral diseases, such as herpes and human papillomavirus (HPV), may be more serious in women who are infected with HIV. The herpes virus enters bodily fluids (called sheds) more frequently and may be a chronic problem requiring long-term therapy. Human papillomavirus, which causes genital warts, has been linked to cervical cancer and thus can become a serious problem for women whose immune system is not fully functional.

The Final Stage

The final stage of HIV infection is full-blown AIDS. People who are HIV positive are said to have AIDS when they are sick with serious illnesses and infections caused by the effects of the virus. Since it is the CD4 cells that are destroyed by the virus, these cells are counted and the result is a rough estimate of the state of a person's immune system. The number of CD4 T cells in a healthy person who is not infected by HIV is 800 to 1,200. Individuals who are HIV positive and have CD4 counts of less than 200 are considered to have AIDS.

Certain disorders have been identified by the CDC as representing a diagnosis of AIDS when they appear in individuals who are HIV infected (see "AIDS-Defining Diseases"). These disorders appear in

AIDS-DEFINING DISEASES

The CDC has identified the following conditions as diagnostic of AIDS when they occur in people who are infected with HIV. These conditions are also used to determine who is eligible for disability benefits.

- Cancer, invasive, cervical
- Candidiasis
  Bronchi, trachea, or lungs
  Esophageal
- Coccidioidomycosis, disseminated or extrapulmonary
- Cryptococcosis
  Extrapulmonary
  Chronic intestinal (greater than 1 month's duration)
- Cytomegalovirus
  Disease (other than liver, spleen, or lymph nodes)
  Retinitis (with loss of vision)
- Encephalopathy, HIV related
- Herpes simplex, chronic ulcers (greater than 1 month's duration) or bronchitis, pneumonitis, or esophagitis
- Histoplasmosis, disseminated or extrapulmonary
- Isosporiasis, chronic intestinal (greater than 1 month's duration)
- Kaposi's sarcoma
- Leukoencephalopathy, progressive multifocal

- Lymphoma
  Burkitt's
  Immunoblastic
  Primary, brain
- *Mycobacterium* species
  M. avium complex or *M. kansasii;* disseminated
  or extrapulmonary
  M. tuberculosis, any site
  Other or unidentified species
- Pneumonia
  Pneumocystis carinii
  Recurrent
- *Salmonella,* recurrent septicemia
- Toxoplasmosis, brain
- Wasting syndrome

SOURCE: Centers for Disease Control and Prevention, "1993 Revised Classification System for HIV Infection and Expanded Surveillance Case Definition for AIDS among Adolescents and Adults," *MMWR. Morbitity and Mortality Weekly Report* 41, no. RR-17 (1992): 1–9.

---

both men and women but not always with the same frequency. They have mostly been studied in men and only recently have disorders specific to women been included. It seems that AIDS is the same in men and women, but there are a few studies to show that there are any specific gender differences in response to HIV infection or treatment. Because many women with HIV have no stated risk factors, the diagnosis is often delayed and a disorder may be severe by the time they seek treatment.

Pneumocystis Carinii Pneumonia

Pneumocystis carinii pneumonia is the most common AIDS-defining disorder in both men and women. It is an infection of the lungs, and symptoms include fever, cough, and shortness of breath. Treatment may be given both to treat as well as to help prevent this disorder.

Esophageal Candidiasis

Esophageal candidiasis is a yeast infection in the esophagus, the passageway from the throat to the stomach. The symptoms can be difficulty swallowing, pain in the chest, and weight loss.

Tuberculosis

Tuberculosis (TB) is a bacterial infection seen in all stages of HIV infection. Populations at risk for HIV infection are also at risk for TB; the current rise in the number of reported TB cases is related in part to AIDS. In early stages, the symptoms are cough, fever, and weight loss, and the disease is limited mostly to the lungs. In later stages of HIV infection, when the immune system is weakened, TB can spread outside the lungs to the lymph nodes, bone marrow, liver, spleen, and gastrointestinal tract.

Mycobacterial Infections

Infection from *Mycobacterium* species occurs in up to 50 percent of AIDS patients, usually after there has been severe damage to the immune system. The mycobacteria are acquired either by ingestion or by inhalation. They then move from the lungs to other parts of the body, causing fever, weight loss, diarrhea, anemia, and enlargement of the liver and spleen.

Cytomegalovirus

Cytomegalovirus is often found in people with poor immune function. It can infect many organ systems, including the lungs, brain, adrenal glands, and gastrointestinal system. Most often, it infects the eyes, causing blurring and loss of vision. It begins in one eye and tends to cause disease in the other.

Toxoplasmosis

Toxoplasmosis infection is caused by a parasite that is acquired by eating undercooked food. It can also be transmitted from cat feces. Initially, symptoms of infection are fever, night sweats, sore throat, and swollen lymph glands. The symptoms can then disappear, but the parasite remains and is reactivated whenever the immune system becomes less able to function. The parasite grows in the brain, causing headaches, seizures, and weakness in various parts of the body.

TREATMENT FOR AIDS

Although there is no cure for AIDS, early medical consultation and medication can prolong the time that a person who is HIV positive can be free of symptoms. In addition, treatment focuses on preventing certain conditions from occurring, slowing the damage to the immune system, and treating conditions as they occur.

Immunizations, such as flu shots, can be given to help keep people with HIV from getting other infections that could do damage in the presence of a weakened immune system. There is also treatment to help prevent *pneumocystis carinii* pneumonia, which is given to people with a CD4 count below 200. In general, individuals who are HIV infected should avoid being around people who are sick, because any infection could be life-threatening, even chicken pox or measles.

Drug therapy is intended to stop HIV from reproducing and destroying the immune system and includes AZT (zidovudine), didanosine (ddI), and dideoxycytidine (ddC). These drugs have side effects and are often changed or used in combination, depending on the person's reaction to them.

Infections and other conditions associated with AIDS are treated as they arise, just as they would be in any other individual. Because the infections can be severe and often recur in people with HIV, however, such patients may need to take the medicine for the rest of their lives.

THE FUTURE

New information continues to evolve about HIV and AIDS and new treatments are emerging. There is no cure, however, and the key to combating the disease is through prevention. Education is the most important preventive measure available. It has proved to be effective in the homosexual population, which through public awareness and educational campaigns has reduced the incidence of HIV infection. The same approach can benefit the general population, where there is an increasing number of women who become infected with HIV today by contracting the virus through heterosexual transmission.

AIDS INFORMATION

For updated information about AIDS call one of the following hot lines.

- National AIDS Hotline: 800-342-AIDS
- Spanish-language hot line: 800-344-AIDS
- Deaf access hot line: 800-AIDS-TTY

Or write to the CDC National AIDS Clearinghouse at P.O. Box 6003, Rockville, MD 20849-6003.

EDITORS AND CONTRIBUTORS

MEDICAL CO-EDITORS

ROSELYN PAYNE EPPS, M.D., M.P.H., M.A., F.A.A.P., is an expert at the National Institutes of Health, Bethesda, Maryland, and a Professor at Howard University College of Medicine, Washington, D.C. She is recognized nationally and internationally in areas of health policy and research, health promotion and disease prevention, and medical education and health service delivery. As a pioneer and leader in numerous professional and community organizations, she served, in 1991, as the first African-American president of AMWA and the founding president of the AMWA Foundation.

SUSAN COBB STEWART, M.D., F.A.C.P., is an internist and gastroenterologist, and is presently Associate Medical Director at J. P. Morgan in New York, where she delivers general medical care, specialty consultations, and preventive services. She is Clinical Assistant Professor of Medicine at SUNY, Brooklyn. Since serving as President of AMWA in 1990, Dr. Stewart has continued to help AMWA shape and focus its mission in the area of women's health.

CONTRIBUTORS

Jean L. Fourcroy, M.D., PH.D., is a urologist with a primary interest in male reproductive endocrinology and toxicology. She is medical officer in the Division of Endocrinology and Metabolic Drug Products of the Food and Drug Administration. She is also an Assistant Professor of Surgery at the University of Health Sciences—F. Edward Hebert School of Medicine and the founder of Women in Urology. Dr. Fourcroy will serve as AMWA President in 1996.

Katherine A. O'Hanlan, M.D., F.A.C.O.G., F.A.C.S., is an Assistant Professor of Gynecology and Obstetrics at Stanford University School of Medicine in California and

Associate Director of the Gynecological Cancer Service at Stanford Medical Center.

Maj-Britt Rosenbaum, M.D., F.A.P.A., is Director of the Human Sexuality Center of Long Island Jewish Medical Center. She is also an Associate Clinical Professor of Psychiatry at Albert Einstein College of Medicine of Yeshiva University in New York. Dr. Rosenbaum is a Charter Member and Executive Board Member of the Society for Sexual Therapy and Research.

Carol Widrow, M.D., is currently an Assistant Professor of Medicine in the Division of Infectious Diseases at the Albert Einstein College of Medicine of Yeshiva University in New York. The major focus of her work is the care of those infected with HIV.

INDEX

Abdominal hysterectomy, 104–105
Abortion, 72–74
Abstinence, 127
Acquired immune deficiency syndrome (AIDS), 21, 22, 49, 65, 142, 148–171
  AIDS-defining disorders, 165–169
  HIV transmission, 149, 151–155
  incidence of, 148–150
  information sources, 171
  prevention of HIV infection, 157–162
  process, 162–169
  testing for HIV, 155–157
  treatment for, 169–170
Acyclovir, 140–141
Alcohol use, 15, 28, 116
Amenorrhea, 93–94
Anabolic steroids, 41
Anal sex, 132, 133, 152, 159
Androgens, 41, 112, 114, 115, 120

Antibiotics, 96, 101, 115, 126, 131–133, 135, 138, 164
Antibodies, 154–156, 163
Anxiety, 9, 11–12, 13, 24, 29
Arthritis, 16
Artificial insemination, 162
Azithromycin, 132–133, 146
AZT (zidovudine), 170

Bacterial vaginosis, 101
Bartholin's glands, 33
Benign prostatic hyperplasia, 111–113
Bethesda System, 51, 76
Birth control, 50, 158
  barrier methods, 63–69
  failure rates, 58
  hormonal methods, 57, 60–63
  periodic abstinence, 59, 69–71

Birth control (Cont.)
sterilization, 45,
71–72, 121, 122
Bisexual relationships,
10, 152, 157, 159
Bleeding, excessive,
95–96
Blood transfusions, 153,
160
Breast cancer, 23, 61, 92
Breast-feeding, 19, 154
Breast stimulation, 8
Bromocriptine, 98
Bulbourethral glands, 45,
46, 49

CA-125 blood test, 82
Calcium, 90, 93
Cancer, 22–23 (see also
specific types of can-
cer)
Candidiasis, 164
Cardiovascular disease,
15, 16, 61, 91–92
CD4 cells, 163, 165, 170
Ceftriaxone, 135, 146
Celibacy, 10
Cervical cancer, 22, 51,
57, 65, 75–79, 165,
166
Cervical caps, 58, 64–65
Cervical conization, 78
Cervical intraepithelial
neoplasia (CIN), 164
Cervicitis, 130

Cervix, 33, 36, 43
Chancroid, 146
Chemotherapy, 15, 82
Chlamydia, 49, 96, 126,
130, 132–134, 137,
138, 142
Cholesterol, 91
Climax, 49
Clitoris, 5–9, 25–26, 32,
33, 35
Colorectal cancer, 23
Colostomy, 23
Colposcopy, 78, 102–
103
Communication, lack of,
12–13
Condoms, 21, 49, 50,
58, 59, 65–68,
126–129, 131,
157–159, 161
Condyloma (venereal
warts), 21, 127,
135–137
Contraception (see Birth
control)
Corpora cavernosa,
46–47
Corpus luteum, 43
Cowper's glands, 45, 46,
49
Cramps, 94–95
Cryotherapy, 102, 136
Cryptorchidism, 115
Cytomegalovirus (CMV),
144–145, 166, 169

Dental dams, 21, 49, 159
Depression, 24, 28
Diabetes, 17, 116
Diaphragms, 58, 63–64, 158
Didanosine (ddl), 170
Dideoxycytidine (ddC), 170
Diethylstilbestrol (DES), 83
Digital rectal examination, 53–54, 113
Dilation and curettage (D&C), 80, 95, 103, 104
Diuretics, 98
Doxazosin, 113
Doxycycline, 132–133, 135, 143
Drug abuse, 15, 28
Dyspareunia, 26, 27

Ectopic pregnancy, 60, 84–86
Eggs, 37, 39, 40
Ejaculation, 44–46, 48, 49
  premature, 27, 116, 118
  retarded, 27
  retrograde, 113, 119
Elective abortion, 72
Electrodesiccation, 136–137
Electrosurgery, 78
ELISA (enzyme-linked immunosorbent assay) test, 155–156
Endocrine system, 40–41

Endometrial cancer, 55, 60, 61, 79–81, 91, 92
Endometriosis, 27, 86–88, 104
Endometrium, 37, 38, 43
Epididymis, 45, 46, 117
Epididymitis, 115, 132
Epilepsy, 17
Erectile dysfunction, 27–28, 116–117
Erection (tumescence), 44
Erythromycin, 133, 146
Esophageal candidiasis, 166, 168
Estrogen, 20, 26, 32, 33, 38, 40–43, 57, 60, 61, 79, 80, 90–93

Fallopian tubes, 36–38, 71, 84–86, 134, 137
Female conditions and disorders, 56–102
Female condoms, 58, 66–68, 128–129
Female procedures, 102–111
Female reproductive system, 33–40
Fertilization, 37, 39, 44
Fetal genitalia, 34–35
Fibroids, 60, 88–90, 104
Fimbriae, 38
Follicle-stimulating hormone (FSH), 43
Foreskin, 46

Gay men, 3–4, 148, 159
Gender identity, 3
Genital herpes, 138–141
Genital warts, 21, 127, 135–137, 165
Glans, 34
Gonads (sex glands), 41
Gonorrhea, 49, 96, 126, 131–135, 137, 138, 142
Guilt, 12, 24, 25
Gynecomastia, 115–116

Health care practitioners, 121, 123, 154, 160
Hemophilia, 154
Hepatitis, 99
Herpes, 49, 126, 165
HIV virus (*see* Acquired immune deficiency syndrome [AIDS])
Homosexuality, 3–4, 9, 10, 12, 21, 24–26, 148, 152–153, 159
Hormone replacement therapy, 91–93
Hormones, 4, 19, 20, 32, 33, 40–43
Hot flashes (flushes), 90, 91
Human immunodeficiency virus (HIV) (*see* Acquired immune deficiency syndrome [AIDS])

Human papillomavirus (HPV), 49, 76, 83, 110, 136, 137, 165
Hypothalamus, 40, 43
Hysterectomy, 22, 78–80, 88, 89, 103–108
Hysteroscopy, 109

Illness, sexual function and, 14–16, 24
Immune system, 162–163, 168, 169
Implants
  contraceptive, 58, 62–63
  penile, 117
Impotence, 14, 17, 27–28, 116–117
Infertility, 69, 89, 96, 117, 126, 134, 137
Injections
  contraceptive, 58, 63
  penile, 116
Intrauterine devices (IUDs), 58, 59, 68–70, 137, 158
Intravenous drug use, 22, 151–153, 159, 160

Kaposi's sarcoma, 166
Kidney disease, 17

Labia, 5, 6, 33
Labioscrotal swelling, 34

Laparoscopy, 71, 85, 87, 105, 109–110
Laser therapy, 78, 88, 110, 136
Lesbians, 3–4, 9, 10, 12, 21, 24–26, 152–153
Leydig cells, 44
Liver cancer, 92
Loop electrosurgical excision procedure (LEEP), 78, 110
Luteinizing hormone (LH), 43
Lymphadenopathy, 164

Male conditions and disorders, 111–120
Male procedures, 120–122
Male reproductive system, 44–49
Mastectomy, 23
Masturbation, 9, 25
Medications, sexual function and, 14–15
Menopause, 20–21, 33, 40, 55, 90–93
Menstrual cycle, 40, 42
Menstrual problems, 93–96
Menstruation, 4, 33, 38, 40, 43
Metronidazole, 101, 144
Mifepristone, 74
Miscarriage, 72

Mittelschmerz, 55
Monogamy, 21, 127
Morning-after pill, 57, 60
Mycobacterial infections, 167, 168
Myomectomy, 89

Natural family planning, 59, 69–71
Nipples, 6
Nocturnal emissions, 33
Nocturnal penile tumescence test, 116, 120
Nongonococcal urethritis (NGU), 130
Nonsteroidal anti-inflammatory drugs (NSAIDs), 95, 98

Older couples, 20–21
Oophorectomy, 81
Opportunistic infections, 163
Oral contraceptives, 58, 59–61, 83, 98, 158
Oral sex, 159
Orgasm, 7–9, 15, 17, 20, 22, 49
lack of, 25–26
Osteoporosis, 90, 92
Ovarian cancer, 60, 81–82
Ovarian cysts, 60, 82–83
Ovaries, 22, 32, 37, 40

Ovulation, 37, 38, 40, 43, 55, 70, 71

Pain, during intercourse, 12, 14, 20, 26–27
Papanicolaou, George, 51, 93
Pap test, 50–53, 76–79, 165
Parasympathetic nerves, 5, 46
Partial hysterectomy, 89, 103, 106
Pelvic examination, 50–53, 93, 165
Pelvic inflammatory disease (PID), 21, 69, 96–97, 132, 134, 137–138
Penicillin, 135, 143
Penis, 32, 35, 44, 46, 47
Peptides, 40
Performance anxiety, 9, 11–12, 13, 29
Periodic abstinence, 58, 59, 69–71
Peyronie's disease, 116, 117–118
Pituitary gland, 40–41, 43, 94
Placenta, 154
Plateau phase, 7
Pneumocystis carinii pneumonia, 167, 168, 170
Podofilox, 136

Postcoital (emergency) contraception, 50, 57, 60, 100
Pregnancy, 19–20, 154–155, 162
ectopic, 60, 84–86
Premature ejaculation, 27, 116, 118
Premenstrual syndrome (PMS), 97–98
Priapism, 118
Primary amenorrhea, 93, 94
Proctitis, 132
Progesterone, 38, 40–43, 60, 63, 69, 79–80
Progestin, 60, 62, 91
Prostaglandins, 94–95
Prostate cancer, 53–54, 56, 112–114
Prostate gland, 45, 46, 111–113
Prostate-specific antigen (PSA), 113–114
Prostatitis, 119
Psychotherapy, 24
Puberty, 4, 32, 33, 40, 41, 43

Radiation therapy, 22, 78, 84
Radical hysterectomy, 103, 107
Radical partial vulvectomy, 84

Rape, 27, 99–100
Rectal examination, 53–54, 113, 117
Rectum, 23
Refractory period, 7
Resolution phase, 7
Retarded ejaculation, 27
Retrograde ejaculation, 113, 119
Rhythm method, 59, 69–71
RU-486, 74

Safe sex, 21, 127, 157–160
Scrotum, 44, 46, 54, 115, 120–122
Secondary amenorrhea, 93, 94
Self-examination, 49, 54
Semen, 45, 49
Semen analysis, 120–121
Seminal vesicles, 45, 46
Seminoma, 114
Sensate focus, 29
Sex therapy, 24, 25, 28–30
Sexual abuse, 13, 27
Sexual arousal, 5–6
lack of, 25, 26
Sexual desire, 5, 33
lack of, 24
Sexual development, 3–4
Sexual expression, 8–10
Sexual fantasy, 9

Sexual function
factors affecting, 11–18
medical conditions affecting, 16–18
menopause and, 20–21
pregnancy and, 19–20
Sexually transmitted diseases (STDs), 21–22, 49, 57, 63, 100, 126, 158, 159
general management of, 131
prevention of, 127–129
types of, 130, 132–146
Sexual orientation, 3, 10
Sexual problems, 23–30
Sexual response cycle, 4–7
Smoking, 60, 61, 76, 90, 116
Spectatoring, 11, 13, 26
Speculum, 51, 53, 102
Sperm, 39, 44–46, 48, 117, 161
Spermatic cords, 44
Spermicides, 58, 59, 63–68, 128, 158
Spinal cord injury, 17
Sponge, contraceptive, 58, 59, 67–68
Spontaneous abortion, 72
Sterilization, 45, 58, 59, 71–72, 121, 122

Stress, 11–12, 24, 28, 116
Stroke, 18, 61
Syphilis, 49, 126, 141–143, 146

Tamoxifen, 15
T cells, 162, 163
Terazosin (Hytrin), 113
Testes, 44, 46, 115
Testicular cancers, 114
Testicular failure, 119–120
Testosterone, 33, 43, 44, 116, 117
Tetracycline, 133, 135, 143
Therapeutic abortion, 72
Thromboembolism, 61
Thyroid disease, 18
Torsion, 115
Toxoplasmosis, 167, 169
Tranquilizers, 15
Trichomonas, 143–144
Tubal ligation, 58, 59, 71, 72
Tuberculosis, 167, 168

Ulcers, 15
Ultrasound, 85, 89, 111
Universal precautions, 154, 160
Urethra, 33, 44–46
Urination, problems in, 53, 56, 111, 112

Urogenital membrane, 34
Uterine fibroids, 60, 88–90, 104
Uterus, 6–8, 22, 27, 33, 36–38

Vacuum curettage, 73
Vagina, 6–8, 33
Vaginal cancer, 22, 83
Vaginal dilator, 22
Vaginal discharge, 55, 100, 101
Vaginal hysterectomy, 105
Vaginal lubrication, 5, 14, 16, 17, 20, 25, 90, 93
Vaginismus, 26, 27
Vaginitis, 100–101, 144
Varicocele, 120
Vas deferens, 45, 46, 121, 122
Vasectomy, 45, 58, 71, 121, 122
Vibrators, 9, 25, 159
Vulva, 5–7, 33
Vulvar cancer, 22–23, 50, 83–84

Western blot test, 156
Window period, 155

Yeast infection, 101, 164